RECOVERING FROM STRESS,
BURN OUT AND FATIGUE

RECOVERING FROM STRESS, BURN OUT AND FATIGUE

Jo Dunbar-Lane

Also by Jo Dunbar-Lane (as Jo Dunbar)

How to Cope Successfully with Candida
(Wellhouse Publishing)

The Hedgerow Clock
Available from www.botanicamedica.co.uk

You can contact Jo Dunbar-Lane at
info@botanicamedica.co.uk
www.botanicamedica.co.uk

Acknowledgements

Many thanks to nutritionist Sarah Noyce BSc(Hons) for her generous contributions towards the vitamin and mineral advice which is so vital in the recovery of health. www.mattersforhealth. co.uk

Very many thanks to Christopher Palmer who helped to prepare the original Kindle version of this book.

My heartfelt thanks to my patients over the years, who have taught me so much and shared their lives, pains, joys and laughter with me. It has been such an honour to know you.

Table of Contents

TABLE OF CONTENTS

Introduction

Let's look at a snap shot of our modern lives: Many of us are so tired that we get up at the last moment, swish down some coffee, then race around the house getting ready for school or work. Dive into the car and zoom off but quickly run into a traffic jam. We are late, so as soon as traffic starts to move we drive too quickly, deftly avoiding the speed cameras. Get to the office, drink several cups of coffee to galvanize our brains into thinking usefully. Some hours later we eat something at our desk, start to feel drowsy so drink another cup of caffeine, work hard to meet ever increasing targets, don't eat a decent lunch so become hypoglycaemic and have a sugary snack. Finally get out of the office. Drive through the traffic to the supermarket, push our trolley around trying to decide what to eat, all the time trying to avoid trolley bashing other exhausted shoppers. Back in the car for more traffic. Get home, if we are disciplined - we cook, if not - it is a ready meal and glass of wine to calm down. See to the kids, plop in front of the television to watch something which is generally miserable or disturbing. Collapse into bed. Wake up exhausted.

Our current Western society places a great deal of value on achieving. We seem to have reached the understanding that to have a happy and successful life you need plenty of money, but you usually have to go through a great deal of stress to get hold of that money. Consider the traffic jams, the commute to work, the targets to be met, flights to international meetings, the very long hours to prove your loyalty to the firm. Once you have made it, new stresses arise - fears of redundancy, school fees, huge mortgage, school gate competitiveness.

How can this be called quality of life? It is largely understood now that although those of us who live in the West have become financially richer, our quality of life in general has become poorer. We spend less time with our friends, less time having fun, less time peacefully in nature. Do we ever feel rich enough to feel secure enough to just enjoy life?

We live in paradise, but we have forgotten to appreciate that.

What is it that makes you happy? Is it the love of your family? Laughter with your friends? Walking in a beautiful garden? Playing with the dog? Baking your own bread? Writing poetry? Strumming a guitar? Jogging through the park early on a frosty morning? Carving a stick in the woods? Watching birds? The freedom to be creative in your own individual style?

Most of us do not take enough time to enjoy those happy moments because in our society we are usually too busy racing around stressfully, trying to earn enough money so that one day, hopefully, we will be able to relax and enjoy those moments gracefully.

A little bit of stress is part of life. It makes life exciting, but too much makes us ill. The aim of this book is to explain how devastating stress is to our health and lives, and how to repair the damage so that we can live peacefully with robust vitality, despite living within a highly stressful society.

PART ONE

How Stress Makes Us Ill

Chapter One

How we evolved to live

Trudy arrived at my clinic today and bought 10 books; the subjects ranged from chronic fatigue, fibromyalgia, food intolerances, migraines, hidden allergies and others. She told me she feels so ill that she thinks she is going mad, because no-one can find anything wrong with her. Tomorrow she has an appointment to see a psychologist in case she is mad (she isn't). She saw her doctor today, who prescribed drugs for her constant dizziness. She told me that he didn't ask her any questions nor even look at her, he just wrote the prescription. She is ashamed of her constant illness, and her husband is beside himself with worry. Last year Trudy experienced severe and unrelenting stress for several months, and now she has hit rock bottom. This is what stress can do to people. Unfortunately the doctor didn't look at her because he didn't have the time to listen nor would he have had much to offer her anyway.

What is stress?

When an over-load of pressure is placed on a material object, it eventually begins to crack, and the object gives way and collapses. Likewise, the phenomenon which we commonly call stress, is our reaction to any kind of over-load which life throws at you. It is the strain of more than we can bear, due to too much physical, emotional or mental pressure. However, sometimes the cracks are not recognized until we actually "hit the wall" and collapse.

We have positive and negative stress, but the effect on the body is much the same. Our body's physiology is not able to distinguish between the good and the bad – only that there is an over stimulation of our central nervous system, which triggers the adrenal glands to release the hormones that help us deal with stress. This is normal and entirely appropriate, except that in the current social environment within which we live, the stimulation is relentless, and our bodies are becoming exhausted.

How we evolved to live

After millions of years of evolution, we finally evolved into Homo Sapiens around 200,000 years ago, very slowly changing our habits, until the last few hundred years when there was a sudden acceleration in learning, bringing us up to date with highly technical contemporary man. If we were able to observe how humans had slowly evolved to live, we would notice that our natural lifestyle involved a great deal of leisure time.

Let's imagine we could peep into a typical example of our ancient life style. It is highly likely that we would see the men hunting or going to war in small parties, and the women growing or collecting the vegetables, doing washing, grooming each other, watching over the children and collecting the water. Note that the clan operates socially as a unit. Everyone works for the whole, and their sense of togetherness gives meaning to their lives. There is a sense of community, dignity and respect. Chores are done collectively, often amid much laughter and at a leisurely pace. They take time for work, time for eating, time to sleep enough. There is a great emphasis on telling of stories, singing, dances and rituals, and plenty of interaction with nature. If there are misdemeanours, the offender is dealt with swiftly (frequently brutally) by the Elders, and balance is restored.

This is how we evolved to live over hundreds of thousands of years – with a sense of community, mutual support, accountability to the group, and movement at a human pace. Of course, living naturally was not Utopia. There was stress, but it was usually short and sharp.

Now, let us imagine that a small hunting party is attacked by a hunting party from another clan – perhaps it is a dispute over hunting territory. Within each person, their brain registers ALARM! The message is sent to the adrenal glands, which instantly secrete cortisol and adrenaline, the stress hormones. These, in turn, mobilize the blood sugars, increase the heart rate and dilate blood vessels, thus driving the body's resources to the muscles so that the hunters are ready to run and escape, or fight their way out of the trouble. This is the fight or flight response.

The event is very dramatic, sometimes deadly, but it is not prolonged. Hopefully the emergency passes with everyone unscathed and our hunting party returns to the clan to tell the story. The rest of the clan might fall about laughing, the context is changed and the stress resolved. Or, the rest of the tribe might plan retaliation, rallying around the victims to collectively support their people. The men are not alone in their world. Their stress is recognized and shared. Notably, it usually occurs as isolated incidences.

Our lives are not like that. Our body's still register ALARM, and go through all those physiological responses to the message, but the difference is that our stress is just about relentless. Our 21st century bodies are registering ALARM several times a day or in some cases, almost all day. Coping with unrelenting stress is extremely energy consuming. Small wonder that so many people in our affluent society are tired all the time.

Even though we are currently experiencing an incredibly steep learning curve which is reflected in our radically changed lifestyles, the evolutionary reaction occurs much more slowly. So whilst our technology and brains are far ahead of the game, our bodies have not evolved to cope with the stresses of our modern days. From an evolutionary and biological perspective, our bodies are still entrenched in ancient patterns, and really struggling to keep up.

We no longer live at a human pace, and our bodies were never designed to live under such relentless stress.

In ancient times, individual groups of people were only in contact with the stresses of their local environment. Without the media, we would not know about suicide bombs in Middle Eastern markets almost every week, see distressing footage of terrorized children of war, or miserable animals in hideous cages. We would not worry about events happening on the other side of the world or even the country, because we would not know about them and consequently these problems would not be ours to worry about.

Although the news today is an integral part of our lives, it does bring an awful lot of bad news right into our homes, every day, without relief. Whilst the media frequently evokes our compassion, it mainly focuses on bad news, bringing relentless and unacknowledged anxiety and stress into our lives.

People did witness violence in ancient times. They would have killed to eat and it is highly likely that they were involved in raids on neighbouring villages or lands, but their violence had a purpose. These days there is so much unnecessary violence on television, and from an early age, most children have become familiar with harsh voices, unkind words, disgusting language and violence as a result of television. Television is what most people do for entertainment after a day of rushing around trying to cope with traffic, crowded supermarkets, demanding deadlines, parking fines, keeping going with sugar and caffeine. This lifestyle is not good for our health and does not support our optimal wellbeing.

We were never designed to live under such stress. Our health and well-being cannot be sustained like this. Although you can survive with unacknowledged underlying stress for years, sometimes just one major or even quite small event is enough to tip you into a long-term debilitating illness which the doctor tells you s/he can do nothing about. That is what happened to Trudy.

Chapter Two

Why am I ill?

When people come to see me, they are often at the end of the line, having seen numerous doctors who, after numerous tests have told them that "*There is nothing wrong with you*". What the doctor should have said was "*I can find nothing wrong with you*". They say that because the mainstream medical profession does not acknowledge Candida over-growth, bowel dysbiosis, or adrenal fatigue in seemingly functioning people. All of these conditions are hugely prevalent in today's society – and they are directly related to stressful modern life styles.

In my opinion, a large percentage of Chronic Fatigue Syndrome or M.E. cases develop out of extreme adrenal fatigue. It used to be called "Burn-out" or "TATT" (tired all the time). Every day, almost all the patients I see are suffering from adrenal fatigue to some degree, and yet they are told by their doctor "*There is nothing wrong with you*". So why do they feel so awful? Are they just imagining it? Are we a society of malingerers? Or is there something going on which has as yet, remained unacknowledged not only by mainstream doctors, but by our very own selves too.

Not everyone I see is suffering from CFS/ME. The greater percentage are professional people, living ordinary lives but who feel as if they are dragging themselves around. They have recurrent chest infections from which they have difficulty recovering, frequent mouth ulcers, cold sores, bloated stomachs, have difficulty conceiving, feel exhausted and debilitated. Their doctors have little to offer them besides anti-depressants, which in my opinion only make you feel better about feeling awful.

Case History

Lucy had recently graduated from university and she was working hard in a company, trying to establish herself on the career ladder. Her bosses demanded long hours, and she found it difficult to find the time to buy decent food. Lucy was ambitious and whilst working for her company, she was also studying for a post-graduate degree. She was involved with a man, but the relationship was inconsistent and this gave her much cause for distress. She really did love this man and tried her best to make the relationship work, for it gave Lucy pleasure to prepare little surprises for him, or occasionally cook him a fabulous supper. He never really went to much effort in return. After 18 months of working long hours, getting up early to complete assignments and repeated break-ups with her boyfriend, Lucy started to notice how very tired she was feeling. Her skin was looking too old, and over the weekends she would either study or sleep. She didn't see her friends very much any more as she was too tired. Life was not much fun.

On week days, it would take at least an hour before she could drag herself out of bed, and she found that she needed to drink 2 cups of coffee before she felt bright enough to function normally. Over the months she became more and more tired. Her skin broke out in eczema, but she was able to hide it with long sleeves. She had repeated headaches, but painkillers got her through the day until she could get home and stare at the television to relax. Eventually she chose to defer her degree for a year because she simply could not focus on her work.

One day, Lucy caught a cold from a colleague and it left

her feeling utterly drained of energy. Although the colleague recovered within 5 days, Lucy still felt unwell weeks later, but she wanted to maintain her record of excellence at the company and did not take any time off work. Three months later, Lucy caught another cold, and awoke one morning to find that she just could not get out of bed. She had burnt out and her body could no longer take her to work. Lucy did recover after some months of herbal and nutritional medicine, during which time she learnt to how take better care of herself. Her boyfriend bolted, of course, but she is now in a much kinder relationship with a man who loves her. She enjoys her work, but keeps plenty of time to do her pottery, which gives her peace and satisfaction. Lucy is expecting a baby soon.

What is going on in your body?

Stress is something which we feel every day, but when there is relentless stress, the body eventually buckles under the strain. In order to understand how stress affects the body, and subsequently our health, it is insightful to understand the physiology of stress – what actually happens inside our cells when we become stressed. Once we have an understanding of how the hormones of stress affect us, we have a much clearer idea of how to repair the damage.

The physiology of stress, in short

When we register or anticipate a stressful situation, the brain immediately sends an urgent message of ALARM to the sympathetic nervous system (SNS). This is one part of the nervous system which deals with our involuntary (automatic) movements such as breathing rate, capillary constriction, shutting off digestive enzymes secretion. The sympathetic nervous system shoots a message down its nerves to the adrenal glands, which immediately release the two hormones of stress, adrenaline and cortisol, into the blood stream. The blood stream immediately delivers these hormones of stress to every cell in our body, making us feel very speedy and agitated. Within seconds adrenaline reaches the brain, which responds by continuing to send ALARM messages to the SNS and the adrenal glands – thus a cycle of ALARM is established, and this continues until the person's brain perceives a reason to calm down.

Once the brain registers that the emergency is over, it sends a message of "all is well" to the nervous system by flicking into the other part of the involuntary nervous system called the parasympathetic nervous system, and the adrenal glands stop secreting adrenaline and cortisol.

This emergency response is perfectly healthy and life saving, but only for occasional short periods of time. Most of us live in a highly stressful world, and thus experience very unhealthy levels of these emergency responses. Some people even feel that they are addicted to the adrenaline rushes. The stress does not have to be stress or anxiety as we think of it. It can be a low grade unrecognized type of stress such as working out too vigorously athletically, living in an unhappy home environment, working excessively long hours or under too much pressure, even falling in and out of love constantly. The cells in the body recognize this as stress. This chronic low grade stress is very debilitating especially to the immune system, and quite often when there is the added burden of repeated viral infections, the house of cards falls down.

For many years I have worked with people suffering from CFS/ME or exhaustion, and my experience is that they have lived busily for most of their life. Consider one man who was in a volatile marriage, with five children and a terminally ill parent to care for, two businesses to run, and his relaxation method was working out hard at the gym. This person thought that he was coping with life pretty well until he caught a nasty cold which was the final straw, and he was eventually diagnosed with Chronic Fatigue Syndrome.

It was not the cold which made him ill – although as far as he was concerned, that was when the illness began. That was only the final tipping point when his body buckled under the strain. The real illness began years before with patterns of a lifetime.

Have a look at the list of symptoms which follows and then we are going to look more deeply at the physiology of stress, so that if you have ticked quite a few of the symptoms, you will begin to understand why you feel like you do. Then we can consider how to get you feeling much better.

Chapter Three

Symptom checklist

If you have several of the following symptoms, especially if you have at least one in each category, there is a suggestion that you may be suffering from adrenal fatigue, Candida over growth or chronic fatigue. A full consultation would be required to make a proper diagnosis, but this is at least a start.

Sleeping and Waking:

☐ I have difficulty getting out of bed in the morning.

☐ I often don't feel fully awake for hours.

☐ I feel tired all the time.

☐ I have difficulty falling asleep at night, or

☐ I feel tired all day, but suddenly feel wide awake and wonderful after 11pm, or

☐ I fall asleep but wake frequently during the night.

☐ I awake exhausted in the morning, even though I slept deeply during the night.

Mental and emotional symptoms:

☐ My brain feels foggy and I cannot concentrate on what I am doing.

☐ I have difficulty staying focused on conversations.

☐ I feel extra sensitive to noise and light.

☐ I frequently have headaches.

☐ I cannot cope with any stress. I either want to hide or I

become very intolerant.

☐ I feel as if I want to avoid people, friends. I just want to be alone.

☐ I can feel tearful for no reason.

☐ I can't cope any more.

☐ I am not ill because I am depressed. I am depressed because I am ill.

☐ I have irrational flashes of anger which I know are unreasonable, but I can't seem to help myself.

Physical symptoms:

☐ I feel bone achingly tired all the time. This is not a normal tiredness.

☐ Every thing I do takes so much effort.

☐ I could sleep all day, but it would not refresh me.

☐ My mind is willing, but my body just won't do it.

☐ My muscles ache.

☐ My muscles feel very weak and tender.

☐ Wounds take a long time to heal.

☐ I can feel very chilly.

☐ I urinate a lot.

☐ I feel shakey inside.

☐ I have shooting pains down my limbs.

☐ I feel tender or painful over my kidney area in my back.

Your reproductive system:

☐ I have lost my sex drive.

☐ My pre-menstrual symptoms have got worse.

☐ I cannot conceive.

☐ I frequently have thrush.

Your blood sugar levels:

☐ My blood sugar levels suddenly crash and I crave sugar, salt or caffeine.

☐ I can wake in the night with a terrible thirst or hunger.

☐ I suddenly feel my blood sugars dropping and I HAVE to eat.

Digestion:

☐ My stomach frequently feels bloated, gassy.

☐ My food remains undigested - like a brick in my stomach.

☐ I often feel nauseous.

Your Immune System:

☐ I have never quite recovered from a viral infection, or

☐ I get colds all the time and find it difficult to recover, or

☐ I never get ill, I just never feel well.

☐ I have frequent mouth ulcers or cold sores.

☐ I have swollen glands in my neck.

☐ I have developed multiple allergies.

Let us look more deeply at the physiology of stress, so that we can develop the understanding about why you have these symptoms, and then we shall discuss what can be done about it.

Chapter Four

GAS and Homeostasis

In the 1930's an eminent and compassionate endocrinologist from Hungary coined the term "stress" to describe the body's reaction to alarm. His name was Dr Hans Selye, and he made it his life's work to understand the nature of stress. Dr Selye observed that whatever the cause of stress, over a period of time, all members of his sample group responded in the same predictable pattern. He deduced that the body responds with a predictable pattern in its effort to maintain life-supporting balance, known in medical language as "homeostasis".

Homeostasis, described by physiologist Walter Cannon in 1932, is the body maintaining its own equilibrium. Our bodies will go to every necessary length to maintain the balances in its cellular environment in order to preserve life. Expanding on the concept of homeostasis, Hans Selye described his own theory regarding an organisms' attempt to maintain life and cope with stress. He named this observed predictable pattern the General Adaptation Syndrome, or GAS.

Homeostasis

Every second of your life, potentially life-threatening events are occurring within your own body, and yet the chemical and electrical balances of our bodies have to remain exquisitely constant in order to maintain life. There are literally thousands of chemical reactions occurring in your cells as you read these words, all geared towards maintaining the constant and optimal internal environment necessary for life – this is called homeostasis. The pH balance in the fluid surrounding your cells, the oxygen-carbon dioxide levels in your blood, waste products from your food, sodium-potassium balance, each muscle fibre needs a precise electrical stimulation from the connecting nerve fibres, your liver is detoxifying every drop of your blood, your pancreas is making sure that your blood has exactly the right amount of glucose, your immune cells are killing millions of invading bacteria, fungal cells and viruses, each nutrient is being absorbed and carefully utilized by the cells of your body, and whilst the toxic matter is sent to the liver and kidneys to be excreted, your heart is maintaining your blood pressure – this is only a tiny glimpse of what our bodies do for us every second of your life. Isn't it a miracle?

For life to be maintained, the optimal balance of the internal environment of the body is utterly essential. Your body is entirely focused on maintaining this optimal balance - homeostasis.

General Adaptation Syndrome

When a person registers ALARM, the body does everything it can to adapt to this stress, so as to maintain homeostasis and life. Dr Selye called this pattern of adaptation General Adaptation Syndrome. The GAS reaction to stress had a predictable pattern, and he divided the pattern into three stages.

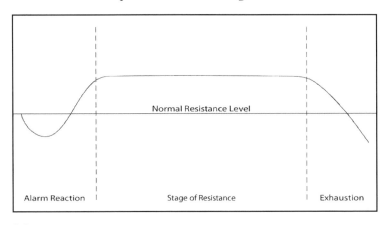

Normal Resistance Level

Alarm Reaction | Stage of Resistance | Exhaustion

Stage 1 - Alarm Reaction: The body is rocked by the shock
A shock metaphorically knocks the person off balance. ALARM is registered. The person recognizes the danger and instantly prepares to survive with the "fight or flight" response. This is all occurring at a conscious and sub-conscious level.

At this stage the brain sends a message via the nervous system to the adrenal glands, which release the emergency hormones cortisol and adrenaline into the blood stream, in order to provide the body with the resources to deal effectively with the danger. These hormones divert the blood from the organs to the muscles, dramatically raise the blood sugar levels, sharpen mental alertness and suppress the immune system. The internal environment or homeostasis is severely rocked by the shock.

This is the stage which our clansmen (in Chapter 1) experienced as surprise, fear and anger when their hunting party was attacked by a rival clan. However, they survived the experience, and got back home knowing that they were safe again. This stage is normally short-lived, and the homeostasis rapidly recovers with little impact on health. These short-term alarms are entirely normal and contribute to the excitement of life.

However, our modern lives are quite different. We experience these short-term shocks, no doubt to a milder degree, at least several times a week, more realistically several times a day, for most of our lives. It is wise to bear in mind that for the body to marshal these resources of survival, a great deal of energy is required. *"Every stress leaves an indelible scar, and the organism pays for its survival after a stressful situation by becoming a little older."* Dr. Hans Selye.

To marshal these survival resources, a great deal of energy is required.

Stage 2 - Resistance Stage: The person rallies and rises to the challenge

If the stress has not been resolved, the body learns to adapt. At this stage there is no outward sign of danger to health, but the body is working hard at maintaining homeostasis. With the unresolved stress, the body is marshaling a great deal of energy trying to resist the stress and survive, but in doing so, is not able to fully recover. The adrenal glands produce higher than normal levels of cortisol and adrenaline, the immune system weakens and so that the body is more susceptible to infection as a result. Sleep is poorer because of the raised cortisol, so rest and recovery is less likely, and the adrenal glands become markedly fatigued.

Quite likely at this stage, we are completely unaware that we are struggling, or more likely, have learned not to take any notice. At this stage, people often use caffeine and sugar as a source of energy, but the stimulant effect of the caffeine pushes the adrenal glands even harder. The person's resources are already stretched to breaking point, and the caffeine, repeated alarm reaction and sugar stimulation push the resources to the edge of exhaustion. Still, the modern person is unaware that there is a bit of a problem looming on the horizon. She usually still thinks she can cope, must push through, and keep going. She drinks coffee to wake up and drinks alcohol to wind down, and our culture is entirely complicit with this lifestyle.

Stage 3 - Exhaustion Stage: Collapse

The person can no longer keep going. She realizes that something is wrong. To have reached this stage, the stress would have been prolonged and the effects of trying to survive it have accumulated to unsustainable proportions. The body's resources have become just about depleted. The immune system is weak now, the adrenal glands are very debilitated and able to secrete very little cortisol. The person is not able to resist or cope with stress.

By this stage the person has "hit the wall", and finally realizes there is a problem. She will be feeling utterly exhausted and wakes feeling as tired as she did when she went to bed 10 hours ago. She is irritable, depressed and tearful, unable to fight off minor infections such as a cold and so becomes repeatedly ill, but recovery takes longer each time. Her muscles may be painful and sometimes she can't even think clearly. In animals, if the stress continues - they die.

So much adrenaline and cortisol has been manufactured and pumped from the adrenal glands, that they have become quite depleted. A scan may reveal that the glands have atrophied by up to 50%. This phenomenon is commonly called Adrenal Fatigue, and it does not describe a normal fatigue. Adrenal fatigue is a deep bone-aching profound exhaustion which is not relieved by a good night's sleep or a weekend away.

I see people with this exhaustion every day in my practice, and when I talk to them about their lives prior to the illness - it is always related to the stressful lives that we lead. Doctors do not have a name or a treatment for this condition. They have no test to diagnose it. The most that they can offer is anti-depressants, which only serve to help you feel better about feeling so awful.

When I treat this condition, I will always be treating the adrenal glands, as well as the nervous system, the immune system and highly likely, the reproductive system, thyroid and digestion too. Before we move onto what you can do about this disease, let us look at the nervous system and adrenal glands, and the effects that stress has on the health of each of these systems.

Chapter Five

Anatomy and Physiology of the nervous system and adrenal glands:

In our modern lives, we have to deal with a great deal of stress. The world seems to be moving very much faster. Women juggle careers, house-keeping and children. Bosses demand that we carry the work-load of three people, men work very long hours, children have multiple after-school activities, university students begin their working lives with a mountain of debt, and our holiday periods seem to have shrunk from 2 -3 weeks to a long weekend away. Most people eat whilst watching television, people drive too fast, we live with the threat of a parking fine every time we try to nip into a shop. We seem to be racing around, spending our lives trying to cram even more into our very busy time-deficient lives.

In fact, busyness has almost become fashionable. You might say that our highly developed left brains have become addicted to stress. The constant race which we live can make us short-tempered, less tolerant, sometimes very rude to strangers, and certainly less cheerful. Unrecognised stress profoundly impacts on our health.

A brief anatomy of the nervous system and the adrenal glands

This section is a bit complicated and maybe even a little tedious, but please bear with it, because it is important to understand the anatomy and physiology of the parts of the body affected by stress, so that you can understand how and why people become very ill through stress or over-busyness.

The nervous system

The nervous system is divided into:

1. The Voluntary Nervous System – controls our deliberate or conscious actions, such as picking up a pen.
2. The Involuntary Nervous System – controls our involuntary or unconscious movements such as breathing, movements of the colon, our breath intake and out-breath etc.

The Involuntary Nervous System is further divided into

a) Sympathetic Nervous System (Fight & flight) – the pathway activated by stress, fear or excitement.
b) Parasympathetic Nervous System (Rest & Digest) – the relaxing pathway.

We are interested in the effect of stress on the body, so we shall focus on the actions of the sympathetic nervous system, which causes the Fight or Flight reaction: When the sympathetic nervous system is stimulated through stress, it:

- Increases the heart rate
- Reduces gastric secretions and appetite
- Constricts blood vessels around the organs.
- Dilates blood vessels in the muscles
- Increases muscular strength
- Dilates the pupils
- Sharpens mental clarity
- Increases blood sugar levels
- Instantly quells sex drive

The adrenal glands

The adrenal glands are part of the endocrine (glandular and hormonal) system and are positioned on top of the kidneys, hence the name ad-renal (ad – above, renal – kidneys). These glands perform a large number of functions, including fat metabolism, controlling inflammation, regulating fluid balance, influencing the immune system, and helping us to survive stress. If the adrenal glands are removed – we die.

The adrenal glands are divided into two zones
The outer zone - Adrenal cortex
The inner zone – Adrenal medulla

The Adrenal Cortex
The outer zone of the adrenal glands provides three classes of hormones:

- Glucocorticoids – Cortisol (The hormone which helps us to survive the stress response)
- Mineralocorticoid – Aldosterone (Maintenance of fluid balance)
- Sex steroid precursor - DHEA (The building block of sex hormones)

The Adrenal Medulla
The inner zone of the adrenal glands provides:

- Catecholamine hormones – Adrenaline or Epinephrine, and Noradrenaline or Norepinephrine.

Cortisol and adrenaline are always secreted when the brain perceives ALARM.

Actions of Adrenaline

- Thumping heart or palpitations
- Anxiety
- Trembling

- Raised blood pressure
- Increased metal alertness
- Quick reaction times

Actions of Cortisol

- Converts the energy reserves of fat and protein into glucose which gives us the necessary fuel to flee or fight.
- Reduces inflammation which helps recovery from injury
- Constricts blood vessels possibly to reduce blood loss in times of injury, and to keep our blood pressure up so that we don't pass out.

The pathway of stress

Now that you have an over-view of the structure of the major systems which transmit stressful messages around our bodies, it is helpful to understand how stress affects us at a cellular level.

When the brain perceives a potentially sterressful event, it immediately fires off fight or flight signals of ALARM to the adrenal glands via the Sympathetic Nervous System. Within seconds, the alerted adrenal glands release the hormone adrenaline (to deal with the event) into the blood stream, and very quickly adrenaline comes into contact with all the cells of the body, stimulating responses such as raised heart rate, and increased blood flow to the muscles, so that the chance of survival is maximised.

At the same time, the adrenaline in the blood stream does a feedback loop to the brain raising the ALARM bells. Straight away, the hypothalamus gland in the brain secretes Corticotropin-releasing hormone, which is quickly transported via the blood to the pituitary gland in the brain, where a second hormone called Adrenocorticotropic hormone is released into the blood stream. The blood transports this hormone to the adrenal glands stimulating the production of cortisol – the hormone which helps us cope with stress. This dramatic cycle continues until the person or event calms down.

The way we live today can be relentlessly stressful, and as a result we secrete far more cortisol than we were ever meant to. Too much cortisol can have a severely detrimental effect on our health. As I explained earlier, with repeated or constant stress, the adrenal glands have to secrete cortisol on such a frequent basis, that it barely gives any time for recovery.

In the early stages of a stressful period in our lives, the levels of cortisol are elevated, reflecting that there is something causing the person stress and the body is able to respond. This is the Alarm Reaction of GAS. Later with the repeated demand on the adrenal glands, the glands become fatigued, and less able to secrete the cortisol - so levels of cortisol are not able to reach the peaks that they managed previously, reflecting adrenal fatigue and the Resistance Stage of GAS. Later, in the Exhaustion Stage of GAS, there is adrenal exhaustion, with the cortisol response being very weak. When I test the cortisol levels, it is not infrequent that the results show a nearly flat line – with the adrenal glands unable to produce the normal morning cortisol peak.

Too much or too little cortisol can affect almost every part of the body. To a large degree, it is the effects of elevated cortisol levels in the blood for too long which disrupts our body, causing unwellness. Or, it can be the effects of depleted cortisol levels which we experience as illness when we have been under too much stress for too long.

The main organs of our body supplying the hormones to help us cope with stress are the adrenal glands. Lets us examine a little more closely, how excessive stimulation of these glands can affect our health. However, before we take a look at the effects of cortisol on the various organs and tissues of the body, it is very helpful to understand how cortisol is produced, because later this knowledge will give valuable insight into why we experience some of the symptoms of adrenal fatigue, and how to repair the damage.

The building blocks of Cortisol

Cortisol is produced in the adrenal cortex by converting cholesterol into a pro-hormone called pregnenolone, which is then converted into progesterone, and finally into cortisol. You can also see from the diagram below that pregnenolone is converted into progesterone, and then into testosterone (the male hormone), or aldosterone (maintains our fluid balance). You will see later, that this is crucial to understanding how stress affects our health.

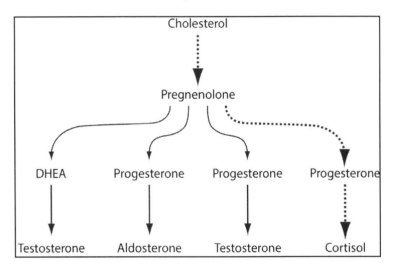

Chapter Six

How stress makes us ill

This is by far the longest chapter in the book, and it includes quite technical matter. You may be tempted to skip it. I would urge you to persevere, because it provides the foundation of what follows, and will help you to understand what you need to do in order to return to health. Please read it in small chunks if you find it hard going.

Almost certainly, our understanding of the effects of stress on our physiology is still fairly primitive; however, by simply looking at the effects of one hormone of stress – cortisol, and the over-stimulation of the nervous system, we can come to the startling understanding of how devastating the effects of stress can be to our health and our lives.

Stress affects the adrenal glands

Books have been written on this subject, so I shall be brief here. As Hans Selye outlined in the early part of the last century, when stress hits us, we tend to be knocked off course for a short period. At that time, the adrenal glands secrete lots of adrenaline and cortisol which helps us to cope with the situation. The immune system is actually stimulated, and very soon we gather ourselves together and get on with our lives.

However, if the stress becomes prolonged, the adrenal glands are compelled to continue secreting cortisol and adrenaline. After some time the glands become fatigued. They cannot maintain this excessive level of stress management. The adrenal glands struggle to support the person but are able to produce less and less cortisol.

At this time the person feels that they cannot cope with any more stress, and this is because their body actually physiologically can no longer cope with the stress.

If the stress persists, the adrenal glands valiantly oblige by secreting what little cortisol they are able to manufacture. Eventually, people develop adrenal fatigue, also known as adrenal exhaustion, adrenal insufficiency, hypoadrenia; or the old fashioned term is 'burn-out'. This condition is characterised by body pain, mental and physical exhaustion, a feeling of brain fog, a strong aversion to stimuli or stress of any kind, amongst other symptoms.

Healthy adrenal glands will secrete a sharp peak of cortisol within half an hour of waking in the morning. This should give us the "get up and go" that we need for the day ahead. The levels of cortisol drift down during the day, so that they are very low in the evening when we prepare for bed and rest. If you measure the cortisol levels of severely fatigued people, there is no peak. An adrenal test can show a flat line with the cortisol levels all consistently low.

Another adrenal hormone called aldosterone keeps our fluid levels in balance by controlling the sodium and potassium balance. Aldosterone is the anti-diuretic hormone, in other words, it holds the fluid in our bodies. With adrenal fatigue, this hormone can also become difficult to produce, and so people find themselves urinating frequently, often a pale and copious urine, and may develop a craving for salty food. It is likely that this craving for salt serves the purpose of holding water in the body when aldosterone is low.

In my practice I see people with this condition every day, yet it is not recognised by mainstream medicine. It is my opinion that adrenal fatigue can be a major fore-runner to full scale Chronic Fatigue Syndrome (CFS), and some studies are in agreement with me in that they consider Chronic Fatigue Syndrome to be a mild form of Addison's Disease, which is complete adrenal failure. Interestingly, liquorice is the old fashioned treatment for Addison's Disease, and this is one of the best herbs to help towards the restoration of healthy adrenal glands, and a major herb to use in the recovery from CFS. In 1998, scientists used a CT scan to measure the size of the adrenal glands in a group of people with Chronic Fatigue Syndrome. In each case, the glands had shrunk by over 50%, which gives an indication of how severely the glands were struggling[1].

Stress affects the blood sugar levels

When the brain registers ALARM, it sends an emergency message to the adrenal glands telling them to to release adrenaline and cortisol so that the body can spring into action and effectively deal with the object of alarm. This potentially life-saving burst of energy requires immediate fuel, and therefore an instant supply of blood sugar is needed whether the person had recently eaten or not.

Cortisol helps to maintain homeostasis, by lifting the levels of glucose in the blood when the blood glucose is too low. Glucose is the most available source of energy in the blood, and in the liver, cortisol converts amino acids (derived from protein) into glucose. From there, the glucose passes into the blood where it is sent to the muscles and brain to use as energy.

Fasting also upsets the homeostatic balance, and the body relies on cortisol to top-up the blood sugar levels between meals and during periods of starvation when blood sugar has dropped. In a healthy person, cortisol maintains balanced blood sugar levels during periods of stress or fasting, thus preventing hypoglycaemia. However, if the adrenal glands have become fatigued, and still the body requires a sudden rise in blood sugar levels, the cortisol is not present in sufficient quantities to perform this task. The adrenal glands simply cannot manufacture enough cortisol. One of the most obvious signs of fatigued adrenal glands, is when the person experiences sudden sugar cravings because their adrenal glands are no longer able to maintain their own blood sugar levels effectively.

Perhaps you have experienced this yourself when you feel that you NEED to eat a sugary snack NOW, and can become quite agitated or even aggressive if your blood sugar levels drop too much. The sugar is actually supplementing your body's ability to supply the necessary glucose itself. Now, once you have eaten the sugar, your blood sugar levels shoot up, and you feel wonderful again – well, for a short while.

When a person eats a sugary snack, within minutes the sugar levels in the blood are elevated to a peak, and the pancreas has to quickly release insulin to bring the sugar levels down to balance again; but insulin is not a precise hormone, and the blood sugar level tends to plummet to very low levels again; thus sooner or later, the person needs more sugar to push the blood sugars up again. Many people live like this, with their blood sugar levels soaring and plummeting throughout the day. They live like a ship in stormy seas, and you can imagine that this is very stressful for the body, which is trying to maintain a homeostastic balance. This type of lifestyle cannot be sustained in the long term, and ultimately something will have to give. If that person does not change towards a more sustainable way of living, then it will be their health that gives in, in the end.

It is often stated that cortisol and insulin work in opposition to each other, and in a narrow sense, that is correct. It is the job of cortisol to increase blood glucose, whilst it is the job of insulin to pack away the glucose into the cells, thus reducing blood sugar levels. However, the reality is that they work together, trying to ensure that the levels of glucose in the blood stream are kept within a narrow healthy range.

It is our chaotic lives which mess it all up. Too much rushing about, too many deadlines, long periods between meals, and then sugar and caffeine to galvanize our exhausted brains into action again. This unrelenting chaos is one of the great stresses in our lives; but then add the stress of erratic blood sugar levels to all the other stresses that our minds and bodies face, and you start to see how much pressure our bodies labour under. Most of the time, we don't even realise that we are stressed, but consider how hard this lifestyle is on the body.

It is the norm in our society for people to live highly stressful lives, and consequently they also have elevated cortisol levels. This means that they probably also have elevated blood sugar levels, and thus elevated insulin levels.

Too much insulin can easily lead to a condition known as insulin resistance. This occurs when your body has been subjected to high blood sugar levels over a long period of time, and therefore excessive exposure to insulin. In time, the cells lose their sensitivity to insulin. Insulin is the hormone which opens the gates in the cells, allowing the glucose to enter the cell. Over time, the gates become less and less sensitive to insulin knocking on the door, and so increasing amounts of insulin are required to pack away the glucose. This commonly results in developing Type II Diabetes, cardiovascular disease, obesity, abnormal cholesterol levels or Polycystic Ovary Syndrome.

Insulin resistance can also affect the central nervous system. Although the brain accounts for only 2% of our body weight, it requires 20 - 30% of blood glucose for clear cognitive functioning. With insulin resistance, the cells in the brain cannot get hold of the glucose required to think clearly, and clinical studies have linked this condition to loss of memory, poor learning, a feeling of brain fogginess, inability to think clearly, forgetting what you are about to do and verbal memory loss.

Another common scenario is that with too much stress, very tired people use sugary snacks and caffeine to keep themselves functioning. The high levels of sugar feeds the yeast cells, commonly *Candida albicans*, living in the gut. We all know from school biology that yeast thrives in an environment of darkness, moisture and sugar – so this is party time for yeast and the population explodes. A Candida overgrowth in the gut can penetrate the intestinal wall with root-like mycelia, entering the blood stream and overwhelming the immune system. Systemic Candida can produce many symptoms which are very similar to adrenal fatigue such as brain fog, muscle pain, and lethargy. This is a drama in itself; to read more about it, see How to Cope Successfully with Candida by Jo Dunbar (Wellhouse Publishing). It is not uncommon at all for people to suffer from both Candida overgrowth and adrenal fatigue.

Stress affects our waistline
You might think that high stress and high cortisol means that fat and protein are going to be burned extra hard for fuel, and you are bound to lose lots of weight. Regrettably not. On the contrary, cortisol stimulates your desire for high sugar, high fat foods.

If you think about it, it is quite logical. You might have evolved to live in a sophisticated city, but your body still thinks that it is living in the bush. As far as it is concerned, any stress might as well be a charging lioness, and that means that it needs to run fast. To get you out of the situation as quickly as possible, instant glucose is required. In an emergency, cortisol converts the protein in your muscles into glucose. However, your body would prefer to preserve the muscles and use food-sourced fuel instead. Hence, elevated cortisol stimulates the intense desire to eat highly calorific foods, which can be used to save you from the lioness. Perhaps that is why some people eat when they are stressed.

Long term stress with elevated cortisol levels has been shown in many clinical trials to be the cause of abdominal obesity, or belly fat. It is well known that people who take steroid medication over a period of time develop round fatty waistlines, and thin arms and legs. This is because the corticosteroids are stealing protein from the muscles and depositing fat around the organs and beneath the skin of the abdomen. This is what happens in the body when we are over exposed to natural cortisol – fat is deposited around the belly and the organs of the abdomen. There is a not very nice description of this cortisol body shape – it is called lemons on toothpicks.

Stress affects our thyroid gland

The thyroid gland is located at the front of our throat, and you might think of it as the thermostat of the body, as it regulates the body temperature and metabolic rate. If your thyroid function is under-active, you feel sluggish, cold, fatigued all the time, and you gain weight despite eating very little; constipation is common and it is also common that hair and skin becomes coarse, whilst the outer edges of eyebrows thin. You can also feel very slow mentally, brain foggy and depressed.

You might have noticed that some of the symptoms associated with a hypoactive thyroid are similar to those of adrenal fatigue. Although these are two separate conditions, it is very common that those who suffer from a low thyroid function not caused by an auto-immune disease, will also suffer from poor adrenal function. To remedy the low thyroid function you first need to restore the adrenal glands. I shall elaborate on this soon, but to understand how the two are linked, I need to explain a few things first.

Your thyroid function can be checked by your GP. Usually he or she will perform a blood test to measure your Thyroid Stimulating Hormone (TSH). The problem is that the range of "normal TSH" is so wide, that even if you exhibit all the symptoms of an under-active thyroid, your blood test results can quite easily result in *"There is nothing wrong with you."* Private laboratories offer tests which test the TSH and the levels of the thyroid hormones T4, T3 and rT3, as well as checking for autoimmunity, so that you get a much clearer idea of how your thyroid is really functioning.

In a healthy person, the pituitary gland in the brain secretes TSH, which stimulates the thyroid gland to produce the inactive thyroid hormone T4. This is converted into the activated thyroid hormone T3 in the liver and kidneys and then enters the cells of the body, influencing metabolism. Excess T4 needs to be cleared from the body, so any left over T4 is converted into another inactive hormone known as Reverse T3 (rT3).

Now, as you have learned, long term stress usually results in adrenal fatigue. The body will always do whatever is required to survive, and considering the adrenal glands are the organs which help us to cope with stressful events, it is now in a position where it recognises that it cannot cope with any further stress. Whereas in the past, the person might have felt tired, but would not stop, there is a theory that now the body takes matters in hand and MAKES the person rest by reducing the hormones which govern our energy. The body insists on regulating its own internal environment in order to improve the chances of survival, and we see this with elevated cortisol blood levels having an effect on the thyroid function.

It is becoming clear that long term stress suppresses TSH as well as T3 [2]. When there is excessive cortisol in the blood, it can down-regulate the pituitary gland's secretion of TSH. Cortisol can also inhibit the conversion of the inactive T4 into the active T3. Further down-regulation of thyroid activity can occur when T4 is not converted into active T3, but rather into the rT3. Reverse T3 is inactive and may even oppose the active T3. It is possible that the rT3 may inhibit the conversion of T4 to T3.

Furthermore, cortisol can also affect the availability of thyroid hormones to the cells. In order for these hormones to take effect in the body, they need to be freely circulating so that they can enter the cells and exert their effects. As the body slows down to survival mode, it increases a protein called thyroid binding globulin, which locks onto to the T3 molecule, making it unavailable to the cells. Like a key which is too large for the lock.

When someone presents me with the above symptoms, I will invariably check the adrenal function as well as the thyroid function. Some practitioners advocate only treating the adrenal glands on the basis that the thyroid will recover as the adrenals recover. I tend to focus my attention on the adrenal glands, but I do also give herbs and nutritional support to the thyroid gland. More about recovering later.

Stress affects our immune system

There is a lot of information available informing us how acute and chronic stress affects the immune system. Much of this information is the result of a relatively new science called Psychoneuroimmunology (PNI). The title has been been expanded to include the endocrine (glandular) system, and is now called Psycho-Neuro-Endocrino-Immunology (P.N.E.I.). This body of science takes as holistic approach as is possible currently, within mainstream science, attempting to look at how stress affects the whole body, and it is greatly improving our understanding of how the mind can cause physical illness, and why stress is so destructive to our health. Of course, I do not propose to present the whole of P.N.E.I. to you, but simply to introduce you to some of the understandings which have been gathered.

Like the rest of our body, the immune system is incredibly complicated and made up of several 'departments'. For the moment we shall concentrate on the part of the immune system called the T-cells. These cells are manufactured in the Thymus gland – hence their name T-cells. There are several types of T-cells, but the ones we are going to focus on are called T-helper cells (Th cells). T-helper cells are divided into Th1 and Th2, which, like cortisol and insulin, work in opposition to each other – thus modulating each other.

Think of them like a pair of scales with Th1 at one end and Th2 at the other. The balance of the scales tips equally between these two, with Th1 raised (dominating) at night and Th2 raised (dominating) during the day. However, under some conditions, the body will be driven either to be more permanently dominated by a Th1 or Th2 response.

The Th1 response gives us the typical symptoms of illness, such as fever, inflammation, malaise, loss of appetite, and withdrawal from society. You can understand now why our cold and 'flu symptoms are worse at night. These Th1 reactions are geared towards killing viruses, bacteria and cancer cells.

Th2 stimulates Immunoglobulin E (IgE). When we have an allergic attack, it is usually because something like pollen or a food has stimulated the IgE to swing into action. Thus we see when the immune system is in a state of Th2 domination, there is a greater sensitivity to environmental allergens.

Now with short term stress, the immune system swings into Th1 domination. This is what Walter Cannon and Hans Selye were observing when they described how the body rallies during a stressful event. This is the Resistance part of the General Adaptation Syndrome model, where the immune system is actually stimulated, and so you may have a cold and experience the usual symptoms such as fever, feeling of illness, but you quickly recover.

As I have said so many times throughout this book, we were never meant to experience stress over a long period of time, and our bodies are designed to experience stress, fight it off and then recover. If the stress is ongoing, the immune scales will then tip from Th1 to Th2 domination, and get stuck there. Over time the immune system becomes more and more exhausted. Now the person is weaker against viruses (low Th1), less able to recover from viral illness, and more sensitive to allergies (high Th2).

Studies are starting to show that people suffering from Chronic Fatigue Syndrome have a bias towards higher Th2 and lower Th1 [3,4], which means that they have higher prevalence to allergies and lower resistance to viruses. This is the time when many sufferers of Chronic Fatigue Syndrome believe they got ill, but you can see that actually, they have been gearing up for this illness for years.

Long term unrelenting stress gave rise to elevated cortisol levels, which depressed the immune system, making the person vulnerable to viral attack. When the virus struck, the body could not fight it off. Ironically, having a viral infection further depletes the adrenal glands, so now there is a vicious cycle. It is not just the virus which needs to be treated but the whole cascade of events leading up to this breakdown which needs to be healed.

It is not only chronic stress which shifts towards the Th2 domination, but also sleep deprivation (caused by high cortisol levels), increased sympathetic nervous system activity - fight or flight (caused by stress and anxiety). Once this shift has occurred, it is not very easy to bring it back into balance.

We know that cortisol powerfully down-regulates the immune system. It is so powerful that the synthesized version of cortisol (cortisone) is used on patients with organ transplants to suppress the immune system so that the body won't reject the organ. On the one hand cortisol is anti-inflammatory, which is absolutely necessary for survival in the case of injury; but this is only useful in the short term. Long term elevated levels of cortisol massively reduce the immune system's ability to adequately respond to bacteria, fungi, parasites and viruses.

Over time, sufferers of CFS have such depleted immune systems that they just cannot fight off viruses or fungi any longer. To fight the viruses, they need the Th1 response which will raise the body temperature. Many invading organisms survive only in a very narrow temperature band and raising the body temperature can be enough to kill them. However, for the body to raise its temperature even 1 degree Celsius takes approximately 10% of our available energy, and, as well as being stuck in Th2 domination (no fever), these people simply do not have the energy resources to achieve the temperature rise.

This is why, the correct herbal medicine and diet are absolutely fundamental to recovery, and why after some months of work, when my CFS patients tell me that they have had a cold – we celebrate. The immune system has 'clicked back' into balance and recovery can begin.

Stress is related to inflammation and allergies

Studies on Fibromyalgia and Chronic Fatigue Syndrome/M.E. have repeatedly found these two conditions to be linked, and to be associated with a disruption in the adrenal gland function and low cortisol levels [5, 6, 7], due to either chronic stress or repeated acute stress.

Long term stress results in adrenal fatigue and the depletion of our natural anti-inflammatory hormone - cortisol. As we saw above, the stress tips the immune scales towards the Th2 bias which is the increase of IgE. Many studies confirm the relationship between chronic stress and atopic reactions e.g. asthma, eczema and hay-fever, as well as increased allergies to foods [8, 9]. An allergy is an inappropriately high immune reaction to pollen, food etc, leading to inflammation of the mucous membranes. However, with fatigued adrenal glands unable to produce the cortisol which damps down the excessive immune response, the Th2 reaction is unopposed, and this may be one of the contributing factors to the increasingly high numbers of allergy sufferers we are seeing these days.

Stress is associated with inflammation in many parts of the body. In Romania, a group of 118 seemingly healthy physicians were studied, and the conclusion reached was that professional stress is connected with inflammation in the body which might be responsible for cardiac disease.[10]

Another study showed that repeated stress leads to inflammation in the walls of the arteries, accumulation of fatty cholesterol attaching to the artery wall, and an increase in blood stickiness. These conditions carry the heightened risk of heart attack or stroke.[11]

Other scientific studies have linked inflammatory bowel diseases to chronic stress, showing that over time, the stress results in a reduction of SIgA (the part of the immune system which lines the gut mucous membranes and defends against invading bacteria). With less SIgA, unfriendly bacteria are able to adhere to the intestinal wall, and secrete toxins which inflame the bowel. A study in Saudi found ulcerative colitis to be significantly related to life events stress.[12]

In Arizona, a study of 58 people with rheumatoid arthritis concluded that greater personal stress had increased an immune chemical called interleukin 6, which is part of the Th2 immunity. This impaired the ability of cortisol to reduce the inflammation as well as being related to an increase in fatigue.[13]

There are so many studies linking stress to inflammation and severe illness. The list above is only a tiny sample to give you an inkling of the havoc stress can wreak on your health and life.

Stress affects our mood

A study cited in a medical journal in 1995 measured the cortisol levels in patients with Chronic Fatigue Syndrome, and in patients suffering from major depression. What they discovered is much in line with other studies which show that depressed people have elevated cortisol levels, whilst in CFS people have lower than normal cortisol levels [14]. This fact lies in opposition to the experience that many have when they are suffering with a debilitating fatigue, and their doctor tells them that they are simply depressed. So many times my patients have said to me *"I am depressed because I am ill, not ill because I am depressed."*

However, cortisol is known to reduce serotonin. Serotonin is often called our "happy hormone" and acts like a messenger to the nervous system. Low levels of this natural chemical are strongly linked to depression. People with elevated cortisol levels quite likely have concurrent low serotonin levels and therefore may experience depression.[15]

Without sufficient serotonin, you may suffer from depression, fatigue, and premenstrual tension, for example. Many people with these symptoms are diagnosed with simple depression and placed on anti-depressants; however, a study in Israel found that long-term stress leads to increased levels of cortisol, which stimulates the white blood cells to take up more serotonin than is normal. The result was less serotonin available for the nervous system and depression is the consequence.[16]

The anti-depressant drugs which are commonly used, are called Selective Serotonin Re-Uptake Inhibitors (SSRI's), and they block the uptake of serotonin so that more of this natural chemical is available for the nervous system to use as a messenger. It is clear to see that this is only the short answer to the long view. If some depression is caused by chronic stress, THIS is what ought to be addressed rather than simply the serotonin levels.

Some of the symptoms associated with low serotonin levels include:

- Fatigue despite enough hours of sleep
- Disturbed sleep
- Carbohydrate cravings
- Headaches
- Loss of libido
- Depression
- Irritability

The SSRI medication may help for a while. However if the stress continues and if no attention is given to the adrenal imbalance then the person's condition may deteriorate. The cortisol level may drop further as the adrenal glands begin to fail to keep up with the person's need for stress hormones. At this point the person may feel increasing fatigue and lethargy. They might find that simple daily tasks become more and more taxing and that exercise, which used to be energizing now exhausts them.

Sleep which used to come easily, may be difficult or they may awaken feeling as tired as they did when they went to bed the night before. Melatonin is a hormone which helps to regulate our sleep pattern, and is derived from serotonin. If your cortisol levels are high – you will have difficulty sleeping. When your cortisol levels are high, your serotonin levels will be low, and so there is less serotonin to convert into melatonin. This translates into poor and disturbed sleep, which leaves you feeling even more exhausted in the morning.

However, if your cortisol levels are depleted, you might sleep, but you will wake in the morning feeling as tired as you did when you went to bed.

High levels of cortisol also directly affect memory and emotion by shrinking a part of the brain called the Hippocampus[17]. This part of the brain is responsible for the formation of new memories and is associated with our emotional response. It is rich in receptors for cortisol, but if too many cortisol molecules dock into these receptors, they start to destroy the nerves, resulting in memory loss, poor concentration and difficulty learning.

A person with depleted cortisol levels tends to become hyper-vigilant and even quite aggressive in order to protect themselves from the stress which they know that they cannot cope with any longer. When upsetting, or startling stresses occur, someone with burn-out finds that they may over-react with anger, frustration, or may startle very easily. They frequently feel anxious but without a reason, and experience difficulty recovering from general stresses of life. Any stress at all 'knocks them for six' and they can take days to recover. No wonder they over-react to the smallest stress - they know that they simply cannot cope any longer. They do not have the resources any more to help them through.

Don't forget how cortisol affects the thyroid, and how low thyroid function is associated with depression. This is why I believe it is so important to really understand why a person is depressed, and why I very rarely prescribe St John's Wort for depression. A person's depression, when understood in its full context after a proper consultation with the patient, will often show to be the result of stress (or despair) and may be linked with a thyroid, serotonin, cortisol or sex hormone imbalance. All of these issues need to be taken into account when treating a patient as a unique individual deserving of a unique approach to their illness.

Stress affects our reproductive system
Women with Polycystic Ovary Syndrome frequently have altered cortisol levels [18,19]. Women who experience pre-menstrual tension have altered cortisol levels [20]. Women who repeatedly miscarry frequently have elevated cortisol levels [21], and scientific studies

are revealing that ongoing stress and raised cortisol levels have a direct and negative effect on male and female fertility.

We often ignore the effects that stress has on the male reproductive system, but a study looking at the effects of stress on fertility showed that common everyday stress such as business dealings, emotional stress or even heavy physical training reduces testosterone levels, decreases sperm count and motility, and increases the chances of impotence or ejaculatory disorders. This study also observed that stress affects women by interfering with ovulation, and causes irregular menstruation cycles and/or early pregnancy failure.[22]

Both men and women who have lived with stress for so long that their cortisol levels are low, are usually simply too tired to think about sex, whilst high stress and high cortisol levels in men can significantly inhibit the ability to achieve and maintain an erection.

Why is this? Possibly the need for individual survival overrides the drive to to perpetuate the genes. Cortisol is a hormone necessary for survival of the individual, whilst the sex hormones are necessary for the survival of the race. In times of high stress (for instance when fleeing as a war-time refugee), the body prioritises survival over reproduction, and will use the sex hormones to supplement cortisol in order to ensure that the individual survives. This is why some women stop menstruating when they are in a drastic situation. The same occurs to some women on long expeditions, or to highly competitive athletes – the body cannot distinguish between fun stress and deadly stress.

It works like this

In men, most of the testosterone comes from the testes, but some of the hormone is manufactured in the adrenal glands. In women, most of our progesterone is manufactured in the ovaries, but a small proportion is manufactured in the adrenal glands. Have a look again at the building blocks for cortisol in the adrenal glands.

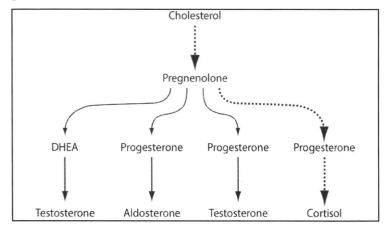

When we are under prolonged stress and the adrenal glands are struggling to keep up with the demand for cortisol, an energy-saving mechanism for the adrenal glands is to steal ready-made progesterone from the ovaries and convert it into cortisol. This short-cut saves several steps in the conversion of cholesterol to cortisol, and provides the cortisol necessary for survival. This is known as "the progesterone steal". It is a bit like eating into your capital when money is tight – it saves the day, but ultimately it weakens your financial stability.

There are so many women these days who suffer from Polycystic Ovary Syndrome, infertility, pre-menstrual syndrome, fibroids, lumpy breasts, pre-menstrual water retention and fibromyalgia. What could possibly be going on?

We live in very stressful and speedy times. Although these are not deadly threats, the body is not able to tell the difference, and reacts as if it is a deadly threat. The constant experience of underlying anxiety severely fatigues the adrenal glands, which have to produce high levels of cortisol in order to cope with the perceived threats, but as the adrenal glands burn out, they cannot drum up enough cortisol. However the stresses keep coming and the body needs to survive. In order to cope, the adrenal glands steal ready-made progesterone from the ovaries, in order to manufacture cortisol to help us cope with the stress. In men, the progesterone is directed more towards manufacturing cortisol than testosterone.

As a result, although there is now enough cortisol to cope with the stress, the progesterone levels start to become depleted. As the female progesterone levels drop, the correct ratio between oestrogen and progesterone becomes unbalanced, with oestrogen levels much higher than progesterone. As you have seen with other hormones, there is a natural check and balance system in our body. Oestrogen and progesterone naturally oppose and balance each other's effects. With the lowered progesterone levels, oestrogen becomes the dominant hormone. This is not the only reason why oestrogen may dominate progesterone, but it is a significant and often unrecognised reason. It is beyond the scope of this book to elaborate on the other causes.

Have a look at the symptoms and see if they relate to you:

Symptoms of sub-optimal progesterone:

- Pre-Menstrual Syndrome
- Fibromyalgia
- Short term memory impairment
- Spasms and cramps
- Irritability
- Anxiety, depression
- Mood swings
- Difficulty sleeping
- Early miscarriage or difficulty conceiving
- Osteoporosis
- Joint pain

These days it is common for women to delay pregnancy until their late thirties or early forties, and by then so many of these women feel "tired and wired" from very busy life-styles and hectic work schedules. It can be very difficult for them to fall pregnant. My colleagues and I have found that if we use herbs and nutrition to support the adrenal glands, these women who previously could not conceive, are often able to achieve a successful pregnancy.

The internet will tell you that if you have oestrogen dominance, you need to clear it with DIM (Diindolylmethane), and if you are low in progesterone, that you need to use progesterone cream. Hopefully, you realise now that neither of these are long term solutions, although they are useful in the short term.

In his mid forties, the male's hormone testosterone naturally starts to decline, which is why men mellow in their middle years. However, the adrenal glands to pick up the slack and contribute some testosterone, but, if a man has been under tremendous stress and his adrenal glands are very fatigued – he literally becomes "knackered". The focus on the body is to produce cortisol at the expense of producing testosterone.

Symptoms of sub-optimal testosterone:

- Lack of love of life
- Depression
- Increased irritability
- Difficulty concentrating
- Fatigue
- Little or no interest in sex
- Difficulty attaining or maintaining an erection
- Development of breasts
- Diminished muscle bulk and physical strength

Stress affects our digestive system

It is helpful to remember that the involuntary (autonomic) nervous system is divided into the sympathetic nervous system (flight or flight), and the parasympathetic nervous system (rest and digest), and that these two systems have a profound effect on our digestion. When we are relaxed, our parasympathetic nervous system dominates and digestive enzymes are easily secreted. The peristaltic movements of the gut move in a coordinated wave-like motion so that we digest and absorb our food easily, and our bowels excrete well-formed stools regularly.

Remember that the body cannot tell the difference between you being late for an important meeting due to gridlock traffic, or you being chased by a potential murderer - when we feel anxious, the autonomic nervous system flicks like a switch from the parasympathetic nervous system (rest and digest) into the sympathetic nervous system mode of 'flight or fight' as it prepares to cope with the situation.

Instantly the blood supply is diverted from the digestive tract to the heart and muscles so that we can run or fight back. At the same time the digestive enzymatic secretions are switched off, and the muscles in the gut tighten. There is wisdom in old fashioned table manners, where it is considered bad manners to discuss religion or politics at the dining table, because it is highly likely that an argument will ensue, which will interfere with digestion, and the appreciation of the food on the table.

When we eat in a hurry or under stress, our parasympathetic nervous system is switched off and so we do not secrete the digestive enzymes as we should do. Without adequate hydrochloric acid and enzymes, the food cannot be adequately broken down and it stays in the gut, feeling like a brick in your stomach. Eventually it starts to ferment, producing gas, a feeling of bloating, flatulence and burping. The "anxious gut" seizes up, and the food is not moved along, but the fermenting food produces toxins which in time can over burden the liver and inflame the gut lining, leading to a leaky gut.

Insufficient stomach acid fails to kill unfriendly bacteria which have been swallowed with the meal, and they now begin to multiply in our intestines, producing very smelly gas, and displacing our friendly bacteria. These unfriendly bacteria secrete toxins which also inflame the lining of the intestine, leading to a leaky gut. Now, undigested food particles escape through these leaky holes in the gut into the blood stream setting up food intolerances, which causes symptoms such as body pain, brain fog and lethargy.

If you live with recurrent anxiety, this state in your guts may become the norm, where you might experience painful stomach spasms, which will probably be diagnosed as Irritable Bowel Syndrome. The cramps and spasms are uncoordinated and interrupt the normal peristaltic movement of the bowels. Faecal matter in the bowel is not adequately evacuated, and the bowels become clogged. Toxins from old faecal matter leach back into the blood stream through the lining of the colon, literally poisoning your system and over-burdening your liver. At the very least, you will have bad breath, but possibly your intestinal lining will become inflamed so that you cannot adequately absorb your food. The poorly digested food passes out from the bowel without adequate nutrition being absorbed, leaving the person poorly nourished, with a liver congested with toxins and even less able to cope with life. I have so often heard people say *"I feel poisoned."*

Shocking isn't it?
This is only the tip of the iceberg. The effect of stress on our body is profoundly disruptive to our health and well being. Long term stress significantly affects every part of our bodies, and yet many of these illnesses are simply treated symptomatically and in isolation. Clearly, treating symptomatically is utterly inadequate because

sooner or later, another more serious symptom will emerge. The underlying cause of illness must be addressed.

When we treat someone holistically, we focus on the whole person, not just the body system which is producing the overwhelming symptoms. That is too simplistic. The long term solution may well be to calm the person, discuss ways of slowing down the life-style, restoring optimal adrenal function, address the diet and particularly blood sugar stability, and then to treat the hormonal imbalances and symptoms. The sustainable solution to optimal adrenal function is to learn to live well. Sustainability is the name of the game.

I propose that stress might be the greatest unacknowledged cause of illness in our age. We must try to address the root of our dis-ease and do everything in our power to live more peacefully. I am hopeful that we might learn to be kinder to ourselves and others, so that we can thrive and live happily with robust health.

Chapter Seven

No-Oh-Noo!

We now know that long term low grade stress, or short term severe stress may lead to burn-out or adrenal fatigue. It is well known that those who suffer from this illness find themselves feeling utterly exhausted after even the mildest exertion. How exactly does stress make us so tired?

Over the years I have often had patients with CFS who tell me that a therapist or doctor has diagnosed them with damaged mitochondria. From our high school biology lessons, you may recall that within each cell float tiny organelles called mitochondria. These are the powerhouses of each of our cells and consequently our whole bodies. The mitochondria produce our energy. It is highly likely that a person with constant fatigue is going to have damaged mitochondria, but the big question in my mind has always been - how did the mitochondria become so damaged? What happened to the mitochondria? If we can understand the means by which they became damaged, perhaps we have a window of opportunity to repair that damage and bring the person back to full health.

A possible answer comes from Dr Martin Pall, a Professor of Biochemistry and Basic Medical Sciences at Washington State University who has suffered and recovered from CFS himself. In his book *'Explaining Unexplained Illness'*[1] he outlines a detailed proposal for the mechanism by which the mitochondria become damaged.

The mitochondria are minuscule organelles found in each of our cells. Within these organelles, packets of energy called ATP are constantly produced and used as energy by the cell. You can think of the mitochondria as energy factories, and the ATP as the batteries which we use for energy.

We use the ATP as our fuel, and these packets of energy have constantly to be replaced. Usually this is something we don't even think about. If we feel a little tired, we take a rest, and then we have our energy back again. People who have Chronic Fatigue Syndrome experience on-going muscle pain following exertion, and they can take days to recover their energy from even the mildest exertion. These people need much much more time than normal to replace the spent energy packets again.

Dr Pall links stress to a little known cycle referred to as NO/ONOO [2], pronounced No-Oh-Noo! Prolonged or severe stress has been shown to significantly increase the production of a chemical called nitric oxide (NO) [3]. Nitric oxide, in turn, ratchets up a chemical called peroxynitrite (ONOO), which stimulates oxidative damage within the cell, and then back loops to re-stimulate the nitric oxide again – hence creating a vicious cycle of inflammation and damage. Remember that the role of cortisol is to reduce inflammation, but if the adrenal glands are depleted and cannot produce the cortisol, then you have an out-of-control inflammatory condition going on in the body, damaging the cells.

Free radical oxidative damage literally wreaks havoc within the cells, physically damaging the energy-producing mitochondrial organelles within our cells. Because the mitochondria are damaged, our ability to produce energy is damaged and in this way, the energy recovery is severely impeded.

Martin Pall further proposes that due to the disrupted adrenal system with shrunken (atrophied) adrenal glands, exercise stimulates the NO/ONOO cycle in a way that is not seen in healthy people. This, he argues accounts for the typical flare up of the symptoms following exercise which is so frequently experienced by CFS sufferers. Indeed, there is evidence to suggest that oxidative levels are significantly higher in CFS patients than healthy people following exercise. [4]

Professor Pall has designed a range of specific nutritional supplements which are highly antioxidant, and these are available through Nutri-Link in the UK. The anti-oxidants mop up the free radicals, thus limiting the damage to the mitochondria. I must emphasize that Martin Pall's theory includes nine other potential stressors, which include psychological and physical stress, as well as infections and chemical toxicity, but as we are only focusing on the effects of normal everyday stress, it is beyond the boundaries of this book to elaborate further.

PART TWO
Getting Well Again

Chapter Eight

How long will it take me to get well?

Usually the biggest questions on a person's mind are:

- Will I ever be healthy again?
- Can I get my life back to the way it was?
- And, how long will it take?

These are very reasonable questions to ask, but difficult for a practitioner to answer definitively, because we acknowledge everyone's situation as being unique, and therefore the time it takes for recovery will vary according to individual stamina reserves, the length of illness, the current conditions under which one lives, and of course the severity of the symptoms.

However, there is a rule of thumb in natural medicine which states that recovery takes approximately 1 month, for every year that you have been ill. But as you know, there is a catch, and that is that your health might have been under considerable strain without you realising it, for years before it actually broke down. Taking all these, and many other variables into account, you can understand that it is difficult to make an accurate prediction.

If you are taking the correct natural medicines and lifestyle approaches, they will start to help immediately, but you may not *feel* any improvement for some time because you are currently so low.

In the beginning of your recovery, there are barely any perceptible improvements (although a medical herbalist will have taken detailed notes and so slight changes can be noted at the follow-up consultation). After a few weeks you may have a few hours or a day where you feel quite a bit better or even perfectly well. This is a wonderful moment because I have noticed that people do finally get to the stage when they always feel this good. However, in my experience, my patient is usually so thrilled with the energy that s/he rushes out and burns up all the energy and then has a relapse the next day. At this point they usually ring me in despair, and I tell them not to worry, but to go back to taking the herbs, and keeping some energy in the tank.

Imagine your recovery like the housing market, where there are dips and peaks, but generally the trend is upward. In the beginning you will feel more fatigued than energized, but after some weeks you find that you have some days when you feel good, and others where you feel fatigued again. Don't give up hope because you will continue to progress to feeling mainly good with the occasional day or hours of fatigue, and finally good all the time if you look after yourself properly.

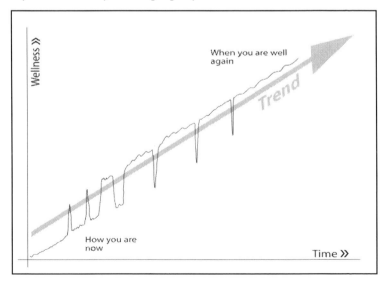

In my experience, people who develop adrenal exhaustion or burn out, are often the type who think they can bust their way out of the illness. "Keep going and it will go away". Unfortunately it won't, because that is why you got ill in the first place. You never gave in. If you don't change these unsustainable patterns of a life time, you will probably remain unwell, I am sorry to tell you. I do say most emphatically, that people do not get better if they try to 'tough it out' or work through the illness. Your health probably crashed because you were not listening to your body, whether or not it was beyond your control. Now is the time to rest up a little, learn to be kind to yourself, and allow others to do kind things for you.

So many times I have listened to my patient's fears that others might think they are lazy or malingering, but in reality, your loved ones are probably only to happy to be able to help you. Now, if they are not happy to look after you for a while, whilst you recover your health perhaps you need to re-assess whether this relationship is still beneficial to both parties.

Having said that – this is not a reason to abdicate your responsibility for your own life. It is important to maintain a cheerful and positive attitude to your gift of life, and a longing to re-engage in life, but just in a way that is much kinder to yourself. I have a little rule in my own life that I fill it as much as possible with "kind things", as opposed to "nasty things". Kind things include a fragrant and candle lit bath, a cup of chai at bed time with a lovely book, supper with dear friends, a home made morsel of marzipan chocolate, snuggling into a super soft baby mohair blanket on a rainy Sunday, walking my dog in the woods, picking herbs in my garden. Everyone has their own version of kind things, and by focusing on bringing as many 'kind things' into your life as is possible, you create your own uniquely wonderful world.

When I say that you need to learn to be kind to yourself, I also mean that you need to do some very specific things which I shall go over in much deeper detail in the following chapters.

1. It is essential that you keep your blood sugar levels even.
2. It is also essential that you nourish your body with highly nutritious foods, and cut out the junk food, which cannot support vibrant health.
3. You need to listen to your body and when you are feeling just a little weary, take a break.
4. Get to bed by 10 pm, even if you don't sleep – just read, write in your diary or knit (etc) quietly. Writing a diary is very good because it brings you back in touch with yourself. Don't forget to count your blessings too.
5. There are specific herbal medicines and nutritional supplements which help to support your health, and I shall emphasize again and again that you will benefit far more from these supplements, if they were prescribed by a medical herbalist or nutritionist who is able to access top quality products, and will prescribe the correct products for your specific health care. Remember that there is never a one-size-fits-all prescription in natural medicine and everyone is treated as a special individual.
6. You need to re-consider your life style.

It is very important is to look at the precipitating patterns which set you up for the breakdown of health, and then to exchange these patterns for healthier choices. Patterns which include pushing yourself too hard have probably been played out for most of your life, and so you can see that change will not happen overnight, nor will recovery occur immediately, because there is a lot of repair work to do. It will take months, maybe even years, to heal the damage. Your recovery is entirely dependent on you changing negative patterns of behaviours and beliefs, but it is at this level that the real healing occurs.

There is another way of living which is much more sustainable. We are all talking about sustainability now. The unsustainable environmental stress under which our planet labours presents a good reflection of the way people are treating their own bodies. Sucking all the oil from the earth, stripping the soil of all its nutrients, and cutting the forests down is unsustainable, and most sane people recognise that it is impossible to continue in that manner. This is the same for your own body and these types of situations insist upon change.

You can train yourself to live more kindly, gently and respectfully towards your own well-being. Your loved ones will notice and hopefully the positive habits will rub off on them, so that this pattern is not repeated through the generations in these very speedy times.

The sooner you start to live in a sustainable manner, the sooner you will enjoy radiant health again.

Before you continue reading, why not glance through the list below, and if you feel that you have a life-time pattern which has drained your energy, take some time to consider how you might adjust this pattern to bring more balance into your life. There are probably other patterns which are unique to your own life that you could add to the list. This is the absolute hub around which your entire recovery program depends – so take your time and add to the list where appropriate.

Patterns of a life time

<u>Unhealthy Pattern</u>	<u>Remedy</u>
I work long hours at the office.	*I am going to leave my desk at 4pm each day*
	....
	….....................
	….....................
	….....................
I am always running around looking after people.	....
	….....................
	….....................
	….....................
I feel at the beck and call of others.	....
	….....................
	….....................
	....

I never stop until the job is finished and
I don't take a break no matter how tired I am. …..................

…....................

…....................

…....................

I am a perfectionist. I will go the extra mile
to make sure everything is absolutely right. …....................

…....................

…....................

…....................

I worry that people think I am lazy.

…....................

…....................

…....................

…....................

I have to prove myself worthy.

…....................

…....................

…....................

…....................

I work hard and play hard.

....

....

....

....

I can't say "no" to going out with friends
even when I am too tired.

....

....

....

....

I volunteer to help because others won't.

....

....

....

....

I take care of elderly parents because my
siblings don't have the time.

....

....

....

....

I have an unhappy marriage/relationship
which is draining me (probably both of us).   …..................

…..................

…..................

…..................

I keep going even when I am ill.   …..................

…..................

…..................

…..................

I go to bed late and get up early even
though it is a struggle.   …..................

…..................

…..................

…..................

I don't take any time for myself.   …..................

…..................

…..................

…..................

I don't know how to relax, I am always
busy.   …...................

…...................

…...................

…...................

When I am tired, I keep myself going
with coffee and sugar.   …...................

…...................

…...................

…...................

I work out very hard at the gym but it
leaves me feeling unhealthily tired.   …...................

…...................

…...................

…...................

*I am going to be much kinder to myself, and allow myself
to rest and do the things which fulfil me everyday.*

*This is **my** life.*

Chapter Nine

Diet and blood sugar

Taking control of your diet and blood sugar levels will have an immediate and profound effect on your feeling of well-being. This is something which is completely in your control and the first step towards regaining vitality.

When your health has failed to the degree that you feel too exhausted to work efficiently (or at all), when you can't bear the thought of interacting with friends, when your body is in constant pain and when you feel jittery and utterly fragile, one of the quickest things you can do to help yourself is to stabilise your blood sugar levels (and get to bed early).

I frequently find that as people start to become aware of their increasing exhaustion, they fuel their rushing around with coffee and sugar. Instead of sitting down to eat decently, our modern culture almost demands that we eat at the desk, or on the run which makes no sense, when you consider that the body cannot physiologically digest and absorb nutrients effectively in the state of heightened stimulation. Not only that, but people frequently miss meals, allowing their blood sugar levels to crash, which leaves them hypoglycaemic. Soon enough they become absolutely desperate for a sugary snack to lift the blood sugars. Living like this is extremely common, and results in the blood sugars spiking up and down. It is very unsustainable and stressful on the body.

Rebalancing blood sugar:

If you are ill with adrenal fatigue, rebalancing your blood sugars is absolutely fundamental to your recovery. If you recall (from Chapter 6), the body considers low blood sugar levels to be an emergency and has to release more cortisol to turn proteins into glucose in order to rebalance the blood sugar. Now, you need to take as much pressure off the adrenal glands as possible to allow them to recover. So, as little stress as possible and nice even blood sugar levels are the order of the day.

From the very first day that you begin to take care of your diet, you will feel the benefits. When your blood sugar levels become stabilised, you will feel as if you are living on much more solid ground. That jittery, hopeless, nearly hysterical feeling will instantly diminish, and the body will welcome proper food with high nutritional value. Don't forget that wise old man, Hippocrates who said *"Let food be your medicine and medicine be your food."*

Let food be your medicine and medicine be your food.

Below I offer some ideas for a typical diet which you might want to use as a template for your healing diet, although I do advise that you seek professional advice for your individual dietary requirements. It is very important that you have your three main meals of the day, with two snacks in between, and possibly a snack at bedtime. Making your meals a little smaller allows for easier digestion and less weight gain. Small, highly nutritious and more frequent meals are easy to digest, keep the blood sugars stable and nourish the cells with the nutrients that they need to recover health.

Please do avoid all caffeinated drinks and sugary snacks, and drastically reduce refined carbohydrates. Try to stay away from highly preserved foods, take-away junk food, and make all possible efforts to eat in a peaceful and convivial environment. If you are upset, your sympathetic nervous system will take over, diverting the blood from the digestive tract to the muscles so that you may fight or flee. When you stay calm, the parasympathetic nervous system dominates, so that your digestive enzymes flow, allowing for proper digestion and absorption of nutrients, thus feeding your body and your health.

Rest & Digest
Diet Template

Breakfast suggestions:
- Poached eggs on rye bread toast
- Sardines on rye toast.
- Sautéed mushrooms and goats cheese on rye bread toast
- Grilled goats cheese on a bed of wilted spinach with a poached egg.
- Tomato and fresh herb omelette
- Porridge oats with a sprinkle of cinnamon powder and half a grated apple, and topped with sunflower and sesame seeds to provide some protein and good fats.
- Avocado pear on whole grain toast with lime juice.
- Kedgeree
- A small bowl of live plain yoghurt, with plenty of fresh fruit, nuts and seeds.
- Slices of tomatoes with raw onions and olive oil on toast, with halloumi cheese on the side.
- Rooibos tea or herbal tea

Snack Options:
- Full fat cottage cheese and a little chopped pineapple or a few dates
- A small portion of cheese and grapes.
- Hard boiled eggs and mayonnaise with chopped tomato

- Discs of thickly sliced cucumber with blobs of hummus on top.
- Alfalfa sprouts with hummus on oat biscuits
- Oat biscuits with chicken liver pâté.
- A few bites of cold chicken
- Cup of herbal tea like liquorice and cinnamon.

Lunch Options:
- Thick home-made or fresh shop bought soup – such as chunky vegetable and lentil, mushroom, chicken and asparagus, broccoli and stilton, pea and ham.
- Jacket potato filled with tuna and sweetcorn mayonnaise, or stir-fried courgette and cream.
- Fritatta or Spanish omelette.

Salad Options:
- Chicken and pesto.
- Hard boiled eggs and asparagus.
- Mozzarella cheese, sun dried tomatoes, and olives.
- Chicken livers, grated beetroot and fresh orange with coriander.
- Proscuttio ham and pears with balsamic vinegar.
- Hummus and olives with olive oil and pine nuts.
- Feta and fresh figs.

Snack Options:
- Fruit with a little cheese or nuts
- Hummus or cheese on oat biscuits
- Cashew nut butter on oat biscuits
- Nut and seed health bars (check there is no added sugar)
- Raw salted nuts (not peanuts)
- 2 dessert spoons of cottage cheese and 2 chopped dates.
- Cup of rooibos tea, carob and rice milk.

Supper Options:
- Lots of vegetables (preferably organic) such as green beans,

fennel, butternut squash, sweet potato, brown rice, swedes, peas, spinach, carrots, beetroot, etc,
- Plus roast chicken, steak, grilled lamb chops, pork chops, home-made beef burgers, etc
- Dal and vegetable curry, or tomato salsa or creamed spinach.
- Aubergine, tomato, onions and courgette baked with cheese sauce, served with spinach.
- Beetroot and radish tzatziki with coriander, and a chicken fillet with steamed asparagus.
- Quinoa or brown rice with roast vegetables
- Sautéed potatoes with garlic and smoked paprika, with fried aubergines and chicken livers.
- Middle Eastern style rice dishes with brown basmati rice, lamb mince or chickpeas, dried apricots, almonds, cinnamon, finely chopped onions and fresh coriander with lemon juice and olive oil dressing.
- Vegetable, prawn or chicken stir-fry with rice.
- Casseroles with vegetables and rice.
- Grilled oily fish (trout, wild salmon) with a salad and baby potatoes
- Good quality free range pork sausages with celeriac mash and roasted baby carrots and beans.
- One or two squares of excellent quality dark chocolate will be absolutely fine, and very nice with a cup of peppermint tea.
- Mix carob powder with some Greek yoghurt or oat cream for a fake chocolate mousse.
- A handful of raw mixed nuts such as pecans, almonds, brazils and hazels on top of Greek yoghurt with a drizzle of honey is delicious. You can add a few cardamom seeds (not pods) for an extra lovely flavour.
- Poached pears or apples with cinnamon, vanilla and cloves over Greek yoghurt.

Bed Time Snack:
- ¼ avocado pear

- A little cold turkey, chicken or tofu
- 2 oat biscuits with cashew-, brazil- or hazel-nut butter
- Organic porridge oats with a little honey and milk
- A little dal
- Hot milk (dairy or non-dairy) with carob powder, or lavender flowers and honey.

A word about salt

Dr James Wilson [1, 2] has developed a range of supplements to support recovery from Adrenal Fatigue, and strongly advocates the use of natural sea salt in the diet. Often those who suffer from adrenal fatigue have salt cravings, a raging thirst and frequent urination. Possibly this is related to the weakened adrenal glands not being able to produce enough aldosterone (an anti-diuretic hormone) and thus unable to hold sufficient fluid in the body. It may also be diabetes, so check with your doctor. Salt helps to hold fluid in the body, and so it is helpful to use sea salt, but not table salt, nor low sodium salts.

Many people with adrenal fatigue describe having an intense thirst, or waking at night with a ravenous hunger. I find that liquorice herb tea with a small pinch of unrefined sea salt significantly helps to hold the water in the body, and the person is less likely to urinate so copiously. I particularly like to use a piece of concentrated liquorice juice stick dissolved in water with a pinch of sea salt. Those who have high blood pressure should not take this tea, but most people with Chronic Fatigue Syndrome or adrenal fatigue actually have a low blood pressure.

If you do find yourself waking at night because of a ravenous hunger, then keep the liquorice tea next to your bed, which you may drink hot or cold, and a fat/protein rich snack. You are waking up because your blood sugars have dropped and your body is in emergency mode. Something like a little cottage cheese, or hazelnut butter on an oat biscuit, or even a small amount of brown rice with some olive oil, lemon juice and a pinch of salt is rather nice – just a small snack will help you to drop off again into the much needed healing slumber.

Herbs which modulate blood sugar

Gymnema sylvestre: Gymnema is a herb from India which is enjoying interest as an anti-diabetic herb. Insulin is the hormone that controls blood sugar levels. The herb acts like insulin, moving the glucose out of the blood and into the cells, and so its effect is termed hypoglycaemic – it lowers blood sugar levels. The value for those who have adrenal fatigue is that is actually reduces sugar cravings, so that you choose instead to eat a lower glycaemic food which does not send your blood sugar levels soaring. However, if you do choose to eat the sugary snack, the herb contains a natural chemical called gymnemic acid which blocks the absorption of sugar into the blood stream. Gymnema should be avoided if you are pregnant or taking anti-diabetic or anti-depressant medication. Additionally, it is thought that St John's Wort, white willow bark and aspirin enhance its hypoglycaemic effects and so it should not be used if taking these herbs.

Cinnamomum zeylanicum: Cinnamon is a bark which is available in most kitchen cupboards. It is a fabulous anti-fungal agent, and very helpful for attacks of diarrhoea. For the purposes of supporting adrenal fatigue, this herb is also one which keeps the blood glucose levels even. Mainly the herb is useful in the case of those who are on the brink of developing any high blood sugar problems such as diabetes.

Nutritional supplements which balance blood sugar levels:

Insulin allows the body to breakdown carbohydrates, fat and protein naturally. When our blood sugar levels are low, it causes the body to call on the adrenal glands to release cortisol to bring the blood sugar levels back up. Cortisol works in conjunction with insulin to keep blood sugar in balance. Every time you eat sugar and refined foods (e.g. white bread, pasta), the pancreas and the adrenals go through this cycle and this puts demand on them. Stabilising the blood sugar levels with nutritional supplements will help to support the adrenal glands, but it is important to get the correct advice from a nutritional therapist before starting any supplement regime.

Chromium Picolinate: Chromium plays a key role in increasing the body's sensitivity to insulin. This in turn will help keep your blood sugars stable.

Magnesium: Magnesium improves insulin response and glucose tolerance, helping to balance your blood sugar levels nicely. Foods rich in magnesium are oats, bran, cashew nuts, beans and green leafy vegetables.

Vitamin E: Vitamin E supplementation improves glucose tolerance and insulin sensitivity. Foods rich in vitamin E are asparagus, bell peppers, spinach and papaya.

Manganese: Manganese is an important cofactor in the key enzymes of glucose (blood sugar) metabolism. Foods rich in manganese are spelt, pineapple, oats, rye, soy beans and spinach.

Potassium: Potassium gives improved insulin sensitivity, responsiveness, and secretion, thus helping to keep blood sugar levels balanced. Foods rich in potassium include bananas, baked potatoes, lima beans, coconut water, tomato soup and prunes.

Zinc: The mineral zinc plays a huge role in your body's production, secretion and storage of insulin. Foods rich in zinc include lamb, oysters, pecans, almonds, chicken and sardines.

Chapter Ten

Sleep deeply and restfully

A lot of people with adrenal fatigue or chronic fatigue syndrome are utterly exhausted, and yet, find that they cannot sleep deeply through the night.

All through the day they feel drained, with no energy, but they keep going, staying up in the evening even though they feel so very tired. THEN, a miracle occurs! The clock strikes 11pm and, PING - they wake up! Suddenly there is the energy that they have lacked all through the day, and so they buzz around getting things done like ironing, surfing the internet, cleaning the house, and they often don't go to bed until around 2 or 3am.

Other people find that they just cannot fall asleep and this is sometimes referred to as "tired but wired", or that they may fall asleep, only to wake suddenly in the night.

My experience of helping people with this illness is that the sleeping pattern can be one of the most difficult problems to crack, but I will relate a few tips which I hope you will find helpful.

Get to bed early enough

Many people who have become ill due to too much stress are goal orientated or achievement driven, and they can feel that they ought to be enjoying evening activities. Frequently people say to me *"I can't just work – I need to have a life in the evenings too"*.

Others feel that although they cannot be very productive during the day, when their brain wakes up at night, they want to use it. This is all completely understandable, but I also argue that until they feel better, perhaps they should listen to their bodies, not their minds. Sometimes the mind is a very hard task master, and the body just cannot keep up.

Do try to be in bed by 10pm with a lovely warm drink, and a gentle book or music to soothe your mind. If you do choose to watch television, steer away from the rampant misery which seems to be so popular and more towards gentler uplifting programs. Do not read thrillers because exciting as they are, they are also difficult to put down. Do not surf the net, which is stimulating too. There is plenty of evidence that the back light from screen suppresses melatonin production in the brain and thus makes sleeping more difficult.

Instead, read something gentle, kindly and even something slightly boring. A lot of people find books on meditation or other such kindly peaceful subjects to be excellent bedtime reading. Then you will find that your mind slows down and by that watershed hour of 11pm, you have dropped your book and slipped into a restful slumber. The idea is that in time this pattern will help to re-set your internal clock. If you allow yourself to become a night owl, the pattern becomes very hard to break and this can become quite an isolating way of life.

Please do be aware that if you have struggled to sleep for months or years, when you do finally start to have regular full night's sleep, you will probably wake in the morning feeling even more tired than before. That is quite normal and it will change. The body has had such a long time managing without adequate rest, that now it is finally able to let go. After a few weeks, the tiredness will lift and you will feel wonderful again.

Sometimes you might feel that your most restorative sleep is from 4am until 8 or 9 am. This is quite a common pattern with adrenal fatigue. If you are able to, allow yourself this time to sleep, but be very careful to make sure you get into bed by 10pm, so that you do not start a new pattern of late to bed – late to get up.

Those who suffer from adrenal fatigue will find that getting up in the morning is a real struggle. They might have to use coffee or tea to kick start their energy and brain, but these strategies will become less and less successful. If you fall into this category, I urge you to seek professional help from a medical herbalist or nutritionist, because this is may be more than just a case of a tad too much stress and not enough sleep. Your adrenal glands need to be restored.

I, myself, have suffered from adrenal fatigue a few times, and at those times, I have been very happy to get home from work, eat supper, run a bath and then get into bed with a book by 7h30 pm! I won't fall asleep for hours as I happily read my book, but I am snug and quiet, and I recover.

Keep a snack next to your bed
As I explained above, many times people wake during the night because their blood sugar levels have dropped. Keep a snack next to your bed so that you don't have to get up and rummage through the fridge, waking yourself up. There is more detail about the snack in chapter 9 about blood sugar stabilisation.

Keep calm but don't carry on
Some people find that they can't fall asleep because their mind is whirling with all the things they need to do tomorrow (achieving again), or worries/excitements of the day gone by. There are ways to cope with these problems, such as keeping a note book which you allows you to draw up a to-do list, so that you don't need to think about or remember the jobs. Keep the to-do list realistic.

Some people even prepare a weekly roster, so that they know what will be achieved , but making sure that some "me-time" has been scheduled into the week. This way, they don't have to worry that such and such won't be achieved, because they can see it will be achieved, but in bite-sized portions. Do make sure that these goals are small and achievable and that you respect your energy boundaries.

As you recover your strength and health again, you can take on more again. I cannot emphasise enough that it really matters that you rest and pace yourself. Give up worrying about achieving. Try to give up worrying. I always tell my patients who worry about their recovery program *"Please don't worry about your herbs and your treatment program. That is for me to be concerned about. Just try to rest, eat well and sleep well. And take your herbs. Try to be happy and think about the things that make your heart sing – then do them"*

Bathing therapy

It has been well known for centuries that water is very therapeutic. When you are exhausted and your muscles ache, lying in a warm bath of water both takes the weight off your body for a while and the warmth allows the muscles to relax. You can enhance this experience with essential oils which can relax the mind, and help to bring about a feeling of strength to the body. Epsom salts are useful to help induce slumber because they are very rich in magnesium which, when added generously to a bath, seep into the muscles, allowing them to relax and release tightness.

Have a warm bath with essential oils and then shuffle softly off to bed. The vaporized essential oils enter the emotional part of your brain (the Limbic system) directly from your nose, with the effect of soothing and quietening the central nervous system. Even if you have lost your sense of smell, the nervous system responds.

Relaxing Bath oils:

Add to 1 tablespoon of base oil (even kitchen olive oil is fine) the following essential oils.

Rose geranium 2 drops
Roman chamomile 2 drops
Lavender 4 drops
Then run your bath and add the oil blend once you are in the water.

Grounding and Fortifying bath:
Add to a double handful of Epsom salts
4 drops of Pine essential oil
3 drops of Siberian Fir essential oil
1 drop of Vetiver essential oil
Drop the whole lot into the bath.

If you don't have a bath, you can use the oil as a massage oil after your shower, or add a few drops of the neat essential oils to a tissue and place under your pillow, or onto a damp cloth over a warm radiator.

A wonderful spa type of bath is to add two handfuls of Dead Sea Salts to the bath with a tablespoon of Kelp powder. It smells gloriously of the sea, and of course the healing properties of both the mineral rich sea salts and the kelp soak into your body.

Seratonin and Melatonin

You read earlier how stress raises the cortisol levels, which in turn reduce your serotonin and melatonin levels. Low levels of serotonin and melatonin will negatively affect your sleep. Some practitioners prescribe 5HPT which is the precursor to serotonin, but this is definitely something you should not self prescribe. Too much serotonin leads to 'serotonin syndrome' which is dangerous.

However, there is a wheat grass grown in Wales which is naturally rich in melatonin – the hormone which promotes sleep, and this is a very safe way of enhancing good sleep. It is called Asphalia and you can take one or two capsules half an hour before sleep. It is very safe to use with herbs or supplements, unless you are already using melatonin, which is prescribed by your doctor, and should not be interfered without his or her knowledge.

Herbs which calm nerves and promote sleep

There are many herbs which can be used to calm the nerves and when I help people, these form one of the cornerstones of the program. One cannot expect someone to recover from a stress related illness if they are so stressed that they cannot sleep.

It can be quite a good idea to take calming herbs in the early evening before supper, so that the herbs have had a chance to quieten your mind some hours before you fall asleep. This is especially helpful if your head is still whizzing from a busy day.

I must emphasise, however, that these herbs are not the ultimate answer. They are very helpful and calming while you take them, and they do have amazing restorative properties, but ultimately you need to put in place strategies to help you cope in the long run with stress. This might include something as drastic as a career change, down-sizing your lifestyle, or as pleasant as taking up meditation classes, or as life changing as seeing a hypnotherapist or therapist for counselling. Some people find that homeopathy or Bach Flower Remedies are very helpful in helping to lift the underlying emotional feelings which contribute or drive the stressful reactions to life.

Passiflora incarnata: This is one of the most popular herbs for those who feel anxious and jittery through the day. It is a safe herb, and leaves one feeling beautifully peaceful. It can be taken in small doses through the day as well as at night to help you drop off to sleep.

Valeriana officinalis: This herb is my favourite herbs to use when people feel overwhelmed with too much to do. When you can't see the wood for the trees, Valerian quietens the mind and allows mental clarity. I have used it several times when someone has arrived at my clinic, red in the face with tension. I give them a fair size dose, and often within 20 minutes they have fallen asleep in the chair. Be aware that a very small percentage people find Valerian makes them even more jittery.

Verbena officinalis: There is a lovely old saying which says that Vervain is as comforting as a mother's hug. This herb can be used when one is stressed and disturbed, but not completely overwhelmed. It helps you to feel more settled and comfortable in your world.

Melissa officinalis: Lemon balm is a very common garden plant which works best when it is freshly picked and popped into a teapot of boiling water. It can work incredibly quickly, and I have witnessed people arriving in a terrible state, and 20 minutes after drinking the tea, are gently settled and more peaceful in their thoughts. It calms the nerves and lifts the spirits. Such a lovely herb.

Scutellaria laterifolia: Skullcap kindly soothes the body and the mind. It can easily be used throughout the day, with the calming effects last well into the evening, allowing the person to have a restful sleep. It is particularly useful if there is muscular tension associated with anxiety. I find skullcap particularly useful when the person feels as if their nerves have been stripped bare, and they are raw and on edge.

Rosa damascena: Beautiful rose - the herb of the heart. Herbalists tend to use rose when the person is agitated on an emotional level. If there is heart-ache, emotional exhaustion and turbulence, this herb rebalances the heart, bringing joy and peace where there was agitation. It combines very nicely with Skullcap and liquorice.

Many of these herbs are easily available, but do bear in mind that you will get what you pay for. When buying herbs, I always emphasise that you should consult a professional medical herbalist who will not only offer the most appropriate herb for you, but almost certainly also include other herbs such as adrenal supporting herbs, immune tonics, etc. Most of all, herbs are the tools of the herbalist's trade and you will judge her according to the results of her treatment, so she will be very concerned that you are given the best quality she can find. Quality is not always the top priority on internet sales.

Nutritional supplements which calm nerves and promote sleep

Magnesium: Magnesium deficiency is responsible for nervousness which can prevent sleep and creates anxiety. Foods rich in magnesium include: Oats - porridge oats, oat biscuits, kelp, wheat bran, almonds, cashews, and brewer's yeast

Calcium: Calcium especially when contained in food, has a calming and sedative effect on the body. A calcium deficiency in the body causes restlessness and wakefulness. Calcium and magnesium taken 45 minutes before bedtime has a nice calming effect.
Foods rich in calcium include: Yoghurt, cheese, broccoli, tinned sardines (by eating the soft bones), chickpeas.

Vitamin B Complex: For those who feel debilitated from nervous exhaustion, it would be a good idea to consider taking a good quality vitamin B complex supplement which helps to support the nervous system. Foods rich in B vitamins includes: Oats – porridge oats, oat biscuits, cashews, brasils, hazels, walnuts and pecans, organ meats such as liver pate on oat biscuits, fried liver and oranges on a rocket salad, egg yolks, brown rice.

Chromium Picolinate: Chromium is often effective for someone with a blood sugar problem that is causing sleep disruption. Foods rich in chromium: Romaine lettuce, onions, tomatoes, brewer's yeast, oysters, liver, potatoes.

Tryptophan: This is an amino acid which is converted into serotonin in the brain, and thus enhances the brain's ability to produce melatonin, the hormone that regulates your body's natural inner clock. Thus trytophan helps to promote a healthy sleep pattern. L-tryptophan is found in foods such as milk and turkey. Milk and dairy products such as cheese, particularly Swiss cheese contains the highest amount of tryptophan available in a food. A glass of warm milk at night, with a little honey and a flower head of lavender floating in it is a lovely old fashioned way of lulling into dreamland.

Phosphatidylserine: This is an amino acid that helps the brain regulate the amount of cortisone produced by the adrenals. It is helpful for those who cannot sleep because of high cortisone levels, usually induced by stress. Cortisone is normally at high levels in the morning, to induce wakefulness. However at night-time, it is found to be high in people with adrenal fatigue, ME or whom have high stress levels. This can prevent sleep. Foods rich in phosphatidylserine: Oily fish such as mackerel and tuna, dairy products, rice, root vegetables.

For your own safety, you are strongly advised to seek professional support from a registered nutritional therapist before embarking on any form of supplement regime. For this reason no amount has been recommended for supplementation. A nutritional therapist should recommend the correct amount for you.

Chapter Eleven

Restoring optimal adrenal health

Restoring the adrenal glands is one of the hubs around which we focus to bring you back to optimal health and vitality after too much stress. This is not something that happens quickly, and it is realistic to expect recovery to take from 6 to 9 months. Before I prescribe herbs for the adrenal glands, I find it very helpful to run an Adrenal Stress test. This test can be performed in your own home and requires four samples of saliva over a typical day. The laboratory charts the cortisol and DHEA levels to show you if your adrenal output is above or below average range.

In healthy people, the cortisol shows a sharp peak in the morning within half an hour of you waking, and this is to promote wakeful alertness. After that, the cortisol levels slowly drift down so that in the evening you are ready to sleep. Some people show elevated cortisol levels right through the day and this suggests continuous reactions to stress. Very often people are so used to feeling stressed that they are not even aware of it, and these results can come as quite a shock.

In time, if you live under constant stress, the adrenal glands become debilitated, and the cortisol levels remain below the average. I have frequently seen adrenal charts where the cortisol is not even able to manage any morning peak at all. There is just a small morning peak, or a flat line which demonstrates quite clearly that the adrenal glands are very debilitated. This is termed Adrenal Fatigue or Adrenal Exhaustion.

Having the adrenal test results can be validating. If you have felt unwell or just plain run down, constantly tired and a bit low, but nothing specific to tell your doctor about, these results can be a real eye-opener. When you have been told for months or years that "there is nothing wrong with you", it is very validating to have a test result showing what is wrong with you. The results alert you to seriously start taking care of yourself, and it is quite helpful for partners to see these results too. Alas, there is little point in showing your doctor these adrenal test results because currently they do not get involved with adrenal health unless you have a cancer or Addison's Disease, although quite likely, dare I say – most doctors are probably adrenally fatigued themselves.

A 5-pronged approach to adrenal recovery

1. Keep your blood sugar levels even and eat highly nourishing foods.
2. Sleep long enough and deeply enough.
3. Use herbal medicines which act as tonics and restoratives for the adrenal glands.
4. Provide the adrenal glands with the correct nutrition, which acts as a building block, allowing recovery.
5. Support the glands with adrenal glandular supplements until they are strong enough to take over again.

Every person who suffers from adrenal exhaustion, chronic fatigue syndrome or 'burn out', will have a slightly different case history, and as you have probably heard many times before – there is no one-size-fits-all program for recovery. It is especially important to bear in mind that herbs and supplements can be dangerous if given in the wrong context, if combined with other medication, or in incorrect doses. Thus I urge you to consult a qualified and experienced medical herbalist or nutritional therapist before taking any natural medications so that you have someone with an in-depth knowledge of the natural medicines, and physiology and pathology, guiding you through your recovery program.

For this reason, although I will mention some of the common supplements which a nutritionist may consider, the foods which are rich in these nutrients are also discussed. Foods are by far the safest and most easily absorbed form of nutrition. Nutritionists tell us that modern foods have low vitamin and mineral values, and if you are severely fatigued, you quite likely are depleted in certain vitamins or minerals, and thus do require therapeutic doses of specific nutrients.

A nutritional therapist will also consider your digestion function too. This may involve carrying out a simple test to assess your stomach acid levels and discussing your symptoms. Having heartburn or acid reflux may not necessarily mean that you make too much acid; it can sometimes be the reverse. Digestion is key to breaking down and absorbing these nutrients from food. Digestive problems are very often also present alongside ME/CFS or adrenal fatigue because digestion requires energy, and that is something that M.E sufferers are rather short of. Highly stressed individuals living in the sympathetic nervous system of fight and flight will also suffer from poor digestion, because they will not be secreting adequate hydrochloric acid or digestive enzymes.

Herbal medicines which restore and tonify the adrenal glands

Glycyrrhiza glabra (Liquorice): Liquorice has long been used to help with the recovery of adrenal fatigue; in fact, it was the 'drug' of choice in older days for the treatment of Addison's disease, which is a disease of complete adrenal failure. This root supports the glands by reducing the need to manufacture cortisol, our natural steroid. One theory suggests that because liquorice root has a natural constituent which has a steroid-like structure, called beta-glycyrrhetinic acid, the constituent behaves in a cortisol-like manner, sparing the adrenal glands the necessity of producing its own cortisol steroid, and thus allowing the gland to rest and recover.

In accordance with steroid like actions, liquorice demonstrates clear anti-inflammatory and anti-allergic actions [1], which is very helpful to those who through periods of prolonged stress find themselves with an elevated Th2 (T-helper cells; see Chapter 6), and depressed Th1 immune imbalance. This immune imbalance is reflected in poor ability to recover from viral infections, and excessive inflammatory and allergic reactions. Marvellously, liquorice is not only a natural anti-inflammatory herb, but also has anti-viral properties [2,3]. These are the reasons why liquorice is an excellent choice for those who are burnt out, with a poor immune response to viruses.

There is a caution, however. Large doses of liquorice can increase the blood pressure and reduce potassium levels, and this herb should be avoided if you have high blood pressure or kidney disease.

Rehmannia glutinosa (Chinese foxglove): Rehmannia has been used in China as a vitality tonic for those who suffer from weakness and anaemia. Like liquorice, it helps to support the adrenal glands; but does not raise the blood pressure. It is particularly indicated for those who feel physically weak, with a sensation of too much heat, or a great thirst. Research has found that Rehmannia may also be helpful in improving cognitive functioning and act as an anti-inflammatory in those with immune system imbalances [4]. I find this herb particularly useful for menopausal women suffering from burn-out.

Eleutherococcus senticosus (Siberian ginseng): Siberian ginseng falls into the category of "adaptogenics". Herbs in this class help us to cope with adversity, increasing our resistance to stress and fatigue. Eleutherococcus comes from Russia, where it was used to help elderly people survive long freezing winters with little food. In these days, herbalists use the herb for those who experience the constant unrelenting stress and invasion of peace, which accounts for most of our lives in the Western world. Today, we know that Siberian ginseng is both an adrenal tonic [5], and immune stimulant [6], and so this is a herb that I might consider for those who exhibit poor immunity such as recurrent colds from which they have difficulty recovering, but at the same time the person feels gravely fatigued.

Withania somnifera (Ashwagandha): Withania comes from India, and according to Ayurvedic medicine, is classified as a rasayana. This term refers to herbs which promote physical and mental health, improve resistance against disease and stress and revitalise the body, in other words, Ashwagandha is also an adaptogenic. Herbalists find it particularly useful for people who have been debilitated for long periods of time. The person may feel weak, easily succumbing to shock or fright with further weakness and fragility. Usually, someone in that state has a very poor libido. Discussing libido may seem as if I am deviating from the point, but a person's libido is a good indication of their vitality or energy levels. If you are too tired or wired, sex isn't going to happen.

A study in Calcutta measured the effect of Withania on chronically stressed adult male rats. The male rats experienced mild, unpredictable shocks to the feet once a day for 21 days. The effect of this stress brought about significantly raised blood sugar levels and glucose intolerance, increased blood cortisol levels, stomach ulcers, sexual dysfunction, reduced cognition, mental depression and reduced immune resistance – all the symptoms humans display with chronic stress. However when the mice were dosed with Withania, their resistance to stress significantly improved [7]. Distressing as it is to read animal studies, this study does show us in compressed time-line just how damaging stress is to our bodies, and how significantly plant medicine can help us to cope with on-going stressful events, as well as recovering from this life-style. *(Profound apologies to all laboratory rats who suffer as a result of the scientific quest for confirmation of herbal knowledge already gained through hundreds of years of safe use)*

Hence, this herb restores energy levels in those who are debilitated, and is also used as a sexual and fertility tonic [8]. Withania helps to rebalance the immune system when Th1 is too low [9], and it is currently exciting attention amongst scientists as an anti-cancer agent [10]. The anti-cancer action occurs by stimulating the Th1 (anti-cancer) arm of the immune system, but also because it induces cancer cell death and acts as an anti-oxidant.

Look at the name – *Withania somnifera*, somnifera means – "to promote sleep". I find this herb marvellously restorative when given at bedtime to people with adrenal fatigue. If given with a little liquorice and passionflower it promotes a wonderfully restful sleep, nourishing the adrenal glands while the person is resting.

Rhodiola rosea (Rose root): Rhodiola grows at a high altitude in the Himalayas, and traditionally has been used to give strength to those crossing high mountains and to protect against altitude sickness. Consider the symptoms of altitude sickness and note how similar they are to long term stress induced fatigue: Headache, nausea, fatigue and weakness, dizziness, sleep disturbance, feelings of malaise, palpitations.

Rhodiola root supports our mental response to stress, and has been shown to reduce cortisol secretion, thus helping to protect the adrenal glands from over-work. Research repeatedly shows that it significantly relieves mild to moderate depression [11, 12], as well as enhancing our mental resilience to stress and fatigue. In America 56 doctors doing a period of night duty were given Rhodiola root. They showed a significant improvement in their ability to concentrate, calculate, and in their memory and general energy levels [13].

Rhodiola protects not only our mental approach to stress, but also the effects of stress on the body. A study in 1994 showed how Rhodiola both reduces palpitations in the stressed person, whilst at the same time protecting the cardiac muscle [14].

As a medical herbalist treating stressed people under everyday conditions, I find this herb particularly supportive for people who are burnt out due to emotional exhaustion and as a result feel utterly drained, fragile and debilitated.

Borago officinalis (Borage): In 1597 the herbalist John Gerard wrote of Borage that it is "used every where for the comfort of the heart, for the driving away of sorrow, and increasing the joy of the mind." He goes on to say that the leaves and flowers, when added to wine, "make men and women glad and merry, driving away all sadness, dullness, and melancholy", and he confirms this information is in agreement with the ancient physician Dioscorides, and philosopher Pliny [15]. Historical herbalist Christina Stapley tells us that Borage was considered so cheering that it was said that a man could watch his entire family being murdered without remorse if tanked up on Borage liquor!

It is used by modern herbalists as an adrenal supportive herb, and a calmer of nerves. We use it for those who feel debilitated and a bit sad as a result of too much stress. Although I cannot find any scientific research supporting its use as an adrenal tonic, the evidence from at least 2000 years ago suggests that this herb is an effective anti-depressant, and gladdener of hearts – and what better medicine than to feel joy in one's heart?

Glandular supplements to support the adrenal glands

Animal glands have been used in medicine to support debilitated human glands for decades, and indeed have proved to be very beneficial, possibly because even though the hormone has been removed, very tiny quantities of the hormones may still found within the desiccated tissues of the gland. The desiccated glandular products thus support the person whose own glands are so weakened that they are not able to manufacture their own. Thyroid tissue has been particularly helpful in supporting those with low thyroid function or a hypoactive thyroid.

I have found adrenal glandular to be very helpful in supporting my patients' adrenal glands whilst we use herbs, nutritional supplements and life style changes to bring these glands back to optimal health. There is a caution, however. Those who feel very jittery and have high levels of cortisol will not benefit from adrenal glandular, because it is supplying, albeit a minuscule quantity of hormone, of which there is too much in the bloodstream. These people will do much better to avoid the glandular therapy and focus instead on herbs and supplements which support their nervous system.

Adrenal glandular is extracted from cows and is called bovine adrenal glandular. The best extract comes from organically raised cows in New Zealand who have never been exposed to Bovine Spongiform Encephalopathy – mad cow disease. Like all natural medicines, glandular supplements have a physiological effect on the body and should be regarded as a medicine, and therefore only prescribed by a qualified natural medicine practitioner such as a Naturopathic doctor, Medical herbalist or Nutritional therapist.

Nutrition and foods to nourish the adrenal glands

Salt: Adrenal imbalance can often leave you craving salt. Most of us are aware that salt can increase blood pressure but low blood pressure (hypotension) is a very common sign of adrenal imbalance. Many people with adrenal fatigue also find that they are extremely thirsty despite the vast amounts of water which they drink, and that they urinate copiously. The adrenal glands also produce the anti-diuretic hormone aldosterone, and when these glands are weak, the production of aldosterone may be compromised, hence we cannot hold our water. One way of helping this is to stir a liquorice juice stick into a cup of boiling water and add a pinch of sea salt. When your adrenal glands start to feel stronger, you will lose your taste for this tea. Please do not use ordinary table salt. Instead use a good-quality sea salt such as Celtic sea salt, or unrefined Atlantic Sea salt.

Essential fatty acids: The reason they are called essential is because our body needs them for good health but cannot manufacture them. These oils support the healing process, and are particularly important for the adrenal glands. They may be taken in capsule form or as a liquid.

Foods rich in essential fatty acids include: Oily fish (mackerel, sardines, salmon, tuna steak), nuts and seeds, flaxseed oil or ground flax.

B vitamins: The B vitamins have crucial roles in the reactions that occur in the adrenal cascade. All the B vitamins in a B complex supplement provide support to the adrenal glands, but B-5, or pantothenic acid, is especially critical because it is important in energy production – severe energy depletion and lethargy can come with adrenal fatigue. People who have adrenal fatigue usually need an extra amount. Therefore you many want to take B-5 as an individual supplement along with a B complex. B-6 should preferably be in the pyridoxal-5-phosphate (P-5-P) form, which bypasses the need for a digestive environment and is much more bioavailable.

Foods rich in B Vitamins: Oats – porridge oats, oat biscuits, nuts (cashews, brazils, hazels, walnuts and pecans), organ meats, egg yolks, wholegrain bread, berries, brown rice, soya beans.

Vitamin C: Vitamin C is very important in helping to support adrenal function. Look for a supplement which contains vitamin

C with bioflavonoids. Bioflavonoids help recycle the vitamin C thus prolonging its functional life.

Foods rich in Vitamin C: Orange or apple juice (check it is not from concentrate), green leafy vegetables, plus broccoli, tomatoes, most brightly coloured fruits, especially berries and kiwis, sweet red peppers.

Vitamin E: Helps to deliver oxygen to the cells. If you take a vitamin E supplement for your adrenals, it should be in the mixed tocopherol form and also high in beta-tocopherols. Because vitamin E is a natural blood thinner, so do not take this vitamin if you take a prescription blood thinner.

Foods rich in Vitamin E: Sunflower seeds, almonds, avocado, papaya, spinach.

Magnesium: Magnesium is one of the most important minerals for your adrenal glands and provides necessary energy for your adrenals and every cell in your body to function properly.

Foods rich in Magnesium: Oats (porridge oats, oat biscuits), kelp, wheat bran, almonds, cashews, brewer's yeast, wholegrain bread.

Vitamin D: While vitamin D deficiency does not normally cause adrenal fatigue, it can contribute to inadequate adrenal function. This is due to the fact that vitamin D increases the enzyme necessary for the production of dopamine, adrenaline and noradrenaline, hormones produced by the adrenals. Low vitamin D may contribute to chronic fatigue and depression.

Foods rich in Vitamin D: Oily fish such as salmon, sardines and mackerel. Eat the skin of your oily fish as it is rich in vitamin D. Look for fortified vitamin D milk. Sun exposure is one important way to raise vitamin D levels. Take time out to be in the garden for at least 15 minutes without sunscreen, on a warm summer's day (watch your skin go slightly pink, that's all you need).

As discussed in Chapters 9 and 10, calcium and several trace minerals like zinc, manganese, selenium and iodine provide a calming effect in the body and also support blood sugar levels. These nutrients can help to relieve the stress that comes with and causes adrenal fatigue, which will ultimately lessen your cortisol output.

Always consult a nutritional therapist before embarking on a supplement regime. No advice on quantity for each supplement is given here for this reason.

Chapter Twelve

Supporting optimal digestive function

In earlier chapters, I pointed out how stress diverts the nervous system away from the parasympathetic "rest and digest" pathway, towards the sympathetic "fight and flight" pathway, causing the muscles in the gut to contract into irritable bowel type spasms, and at the same time cutting off the flow of digestive acids and enzymes. When we eat stressfully, food is gulped down instead of being thoroughly chewed and mixed with the saliva. These large chunks hit the stomach, but without sufficient acid in the stomach and enzymes in the small intestine, the food does not digest sufficiently. It feels like a brick in the stomach because it is not broken down. The food begins to ferment, producing lots of gas and the person feels bloated, gassy and uncomfortable. Within the gut, the environment becomes conducive to the over-growth of unfriendly bacteria, producing toxins as a by product of their life cycles. These toxins inflame the gut lining, leading to increased gut permeability, which is when the gaps in the intestinal lining become enlarged like a leaky hose-pipe, allowing undigested food particles to escape into the bloodstream.

Because the person is not absorbing nutrients and is feeling so tired, they might eat sugar to give them energy. It is quite normal for yeast to live in small populations in our guts, but when too much sugar is added to the dark, moist environment of the gut, the yeast population absolutely explodes. (Think how quickly a mushroom can pop up on the lawn overnight.) These yeasts quickly grow root-like mycelia, which penetrate the gut wall, causing further gut permeability (leaky gut). Now the undigested food particles and the yeast cells are able to escape through the gaps in the gut wall into the blood stream. But the patrolling immune system in the blood does not recognise these large undigested food particles and instantly starts to attack them, because that is its job. It becomes sensitised to these foods and so food intolerances develop.

As a result of always having to attack the food particles and yeasts, the immune system becomes very tired, but at the same time the high levels of cortisol are damping down the immune response. The exhausted immune system starts to confuse the body's own tissues with the large particles of food proteins which should not be floating about in the blood stream, and so it begins to attack the body tissues as well – often resulting in joint pains. The yeast cells progress into the joints, depositing toxins, furthering the joint pain. They progress into the brain, causing brain fog. They also progress into the sinuses, causing sinus congestion. The person who owns this body becomes more and more tired, head-achy, and frequently resorts to sugar and caffeine to keep going.

Such a familiar story and such a scary outcome.

The damage caused by stress is devastating to the body, but, it is repairable. Once again, I will say that you are strongly advised to see a medical herbalist or nutritionist if you think you are suffering from Candida or leaky gut. However, there is a great deal that you can do yourself to heal your own body. Below, I am going to mention foods and herbal teas which you can use to heal your own gut, and these can go a long way toward fully repairing your health. This is how you do it.

Healing your digestive system
1. Rest and Digest.
2. Relax the gut.
3. Encourage the flow of digestive enzymes.
4. Encourage regular bowel movements and clear the bowels.
5. Support the liver.

6. Kill any Candida.
7. Probiotics and prebiotics.
8. Heal the leaky gut.
9. Have a food intolerance test.

Rest and Digest

We were not designed to eat on the hoof. When do you ever see a Bushman running whilst eating his steak? Never! He has the good sense to sit down with his family and tell wonderful stories while he eats his food at a leisurely pace. In doing so, he allows the correct pathway of his nervous system to prepare his gut to digest his food.

We don't have the luxury of time in our money-rich, time-poor lives, but do try your very best to endeavour to eat in a civilized manner. Not long ago we all sat down to eat as a family at a regular time, at the dining room table. We did not take phone calls or watch television, and arguments were strongly discouraged. There was a lot of wisdom in that.

Many of us don't have dining rooms any more, but we can prepare our own food, the smells of which already get our digestive systems into the mood. The slowness of cooking is in itself a quiet time. Then sitting with your family or friends, with gentle music, candles if you wish, and convivial conversation is a civilized way to eat. Chew slowly and eat peacefully. You eat less in this way and lose weight, as an added bonus.

Relax the gut

Many people don't show their stress or anxiety, but feel it acutely in their guts. There are wonderful herbs which really help to relax the powerful and very painful spasms in the muscles which surround our intestines. These teas are readily available, and can even be grown in your garden.

German chamomile, Roman chamomile, fennel, peppermint or spearmint and ginger are all simple and absolutely fabulous at relaxing the tight cramping stomach muscles, and in doing so, they help to encourage the secretions of digestive enzymes. It is terribly easy to make a very effective tea.

Tummy Tea:
1 bag of chamomile tea
2 sprigs of fresh mint
1 tsp of fennel or caraway seeds
5 slices of fresh ginger root
1 slice of lemon
a little honey if you wish.

Pop these into a tea pot and allow to brew for 10 minutes. Then strain and sip gently whilst relaxing. Perhaps you could make a ritual of it with deeply relaxing music, or lying on your bed with a magazine and soft lighting. Make a special moment of your herb tea.

Encourage digestive enzymes

Even in the last century it was not uncommon that when you ate a meal at a hotel, you were given a small glass of pineapple juice or half a grapefruit as a starter. This is not just a social nicety, but the fruit juices send a message to your stomach that it needs to start releasing digestive enzymes now. So these fruit juices encouraged digestion.

You can take the full range of digestive enzymes at the start of each meal if you have real trouble digesting your food, and some people with CFS/ME are so debilitated that their bodies do not even have the energy to digest their food. Then, digestive enzymes are a must for a while, but for those who are run down and trying to avoid going into complete burn-out, you can either follow the social niceties of hotels in the 20th century, or add 1 tablespoon of apple cider vinegar to half a glass of warm water and drink that before each meal. Other options to consider:

1. Add half a lemon squeezed into half a glass of water and sip for half an hour before a meal.
2. Bitter foods such as rocket, radishes or chicory salad will help secrete digestive enzymes, so try adding some to your salad mix.
3. Fragrant herbs such as thyme, oregano and sage also encourage the secretion of digestive enzymes and these can be added to salads or casseroles.
4. A common plant digestive enzyme other than Bromelain (found in pineapples), is Papain, found in paw-paw. These enzymes are especially good at breaking down and digesting proteins. Try having a small portion just before a meal.

People ill with ME/CFS or adrenal fatigue can often have digestive problems, which may include not producing enough hydrochloric acid (stomach acid). Hydrochloric acid helps with the breakdown and absorption of nutrients such as calcium or iron, and to control the growth of unwanted bacterias in the digestive tract. We can feel bloated, gassy, full or even have heartburn, with low levels of hydrochloric acid in our stomach. Bitter herbs may stimulate the secretion of stomach acid and digestive enzymes. Examples of bitter herbs are gentian and dandelion. They are often recommended in liquid vs. capsule form because it's the bitter taste that's thought to trigger the release of digestive juices.

Encourage regular bowel movements and clear the bowels

When stress affects the small and large colons, it causes them to seize up, because the muscles tighten with anxiety. In the old days this used to be called spastic colon. If the large bowel does not contract and empty the faecal matter regularly, the toxins in the faeces starts to leach back through the colon, inflaming the intestinal lining, and leading to toxins being deposited in the cells. The liver becomes clogged up, leading to poor detoxification of the blood, headaches, lethargy and bad skin.

The bowel needs to be relaxed, and that is what we have discussed above, but it also needs to be encouraged to empty. If there is enough roughage and fluid in the contents of the faeces, these will swell slightly, causing the walls of the large intestine to be gently dilated. This gentle stretch stimulates the muscles of the bowel to contract in a co-ordinated manner, in other words, it will stimulate a bowel movement.

One of the simplest and best ways of encouraging a bowel movement is to include linseeds in the diet. When the linseeds are introduced to the gut they absorb the fluid in the digestive tract, and also trap any toxins which have been eliminated by the bile from the liver. Then this lovely slimy roughage swells in the bowel, encouraging an enormous bowel movement, and you experience a wonderful feeling of complete emptying.

Linseed yoghurt
In a cup of live plain yoghurt, add 1 or 2 dessert spoons of linseeds. Eat this every day, at any time of the day. You may add if you wish, some prunes, or fruit or even carob powder. Then it is very important that you immediately follow this with a large glass of warm water or herbal tea as described above.

Support the liver
Liver support is always appropriate, because it is the major organ of detoxification in the body, and hence, could always do with a little help.

Located just under the ribcage on the right side of the abdomen, the liver is the largest and one of the most important organs in the human body. It performs hundreds of tasks in every minute of everyday – more than any other organ, including the brain! It is constantly filtering, detoxifying, synthesizing, and processing a wide variety of substances. These may consist of physiological substances e.g. hormones, bacterial overgrowth; or external substances e.g. car fumes or cigarette smoke.

It also has to deal with emotions too believe it or not, so stress puts an extra burden on the liver.

Without a healthy, well-functioning liver, it is easy to become overly-toxic, which can lead to chronic fatigue, a general feeling of sickness and depression. In addition to its endless detoxification work, the liver is also an organ that produces energy to our bodies. It does so by regulating carbohydrate and protein metabolism, hormonal activity, fat burning and blood sugar control. It is also closely linked to your digestion, and secretes bile into your small intestine. The bile secreted by your liver separates the fats that you eat so that they can be broken down by enzymes. Some of our patients can complain of a feeling of 'not being able to digest fat'. This may be a reflection of the liver and gallbladder in need of support. Herbs and foods can nicely support the gallbladder and liver when fat digestion becomes a problem.

Tips to support a healthy liver
1. Try having a hot glass of water, with a slice of lemon steeped in it, first thing in the morning. Sip it gently. This 'kick-starts' the liver and helps encourage digestive enzymes.
2. If possible, choose organic foods to eliminate pesticide toxins. This also includes eating free-range meats and eggs where possible and within budget.
3. Healthy grains such as brown rice and quinoa are rich in B-complex vitamins, which improve overall fat metabolism, liver function and liver de-congestion.
4. Suspend, at least temporarily, the use of alcohol, coffee, soft drinks and refined sugar of any kind.

5. Drink water daily, such as 6-8 glasses.
6. Garlic has the ability to activate the liver enzymes that help your body flush out toxins. Garlic also holds high amounts of allicin and selenium, two natural compounds that aid in liver cleansing, and at the same time it is a fabulous anti-fungal, antibacterial and anti-viral vegetable.
7. Grapefruit is high in both vitamin C and anti-oxidants; grapefruit increases the natural cleansing processes of the liver. A small glass of freshly squeezed grapefruit juice will help boost production of liver detoxification enzymes that help flush toxins.
8. Beetroot and carrots are both extremely high in plant flavonoids and beta-carotene. Eating both beetroot and carrots can help stimulate and improve overall liver function.
9. Green tea – this liver-loving beverage is bursting with plant antioxidants known as catechins, a constituent known to assist the livers overall functions.
10. Leafy green vegetables are our most powerful allies in cleansing the liver. Leafy greens can be eaten raw, cooked or juiced. Extremely high in plant chlorophylls, greens literally suck up environmental toxins from the blood stream. With their distinct ability to neutralize heavy metals, chemicals and pesticides, these cleansing foods offer a powerful protective mechanism for the liver.
11. Avocados are nutrient-dense super-food, which help the body produce glutathione, necessary for the liver to cleanse harmful toxins.
12. Apples are high in pectin, and hold the chemical constituents needed for the body to cleanse and release toxins from the digestive tract. This, in turn, makes it easier for the liver to handle the toxic load in the body.
13. Walnuts are high in glutathione and omega-3 fatty acids, which support normal liver cleansing actions. Make sure you chew the nuts well (until they are liquefied) before swallowing.

Liver supporting herbs have been discussed several times in this book. Some excellent liver herbs include dandelion root, milk thistle, ginger root and tumeric root.

Kill yeast over-growth

Candidiasis is one of those "diagnoses" which became terribly fashionable about 10 years ago. Since those who suffer with Candida do have a wide range of symptoms, almost everyone with any symptom was "diagnosed" with Candida. Do check if you have actually have Candida before going on a strict anti-fungal diet. Personally, I do not think much of the "spit into a glass of water" test. There are laboratory saliva tests available which are accurate and reliable, and do not cost so much that it is not worth the price.

If you do find out that you have a Candida overgrowth, then you should take strong action, because it can only lead to further ill health and it needs to be resolved. See (*How to cope successfully with Candida*, Jo Dunbar, Wellhouse Publishing) where I have written at length about this illness.

At the very least, you have to avoid all sugar, and that includes agave syrup, honey, protea nectar, biscuits, sweets, fizzy drinks, wine and refined carbohydrates. This starves and weakens the yeast, but that is not enough. The Candida yeast is a very resourceful character and will find a way to turn any food to its own benefit, so you need to use anti-fungal agents to kill it.

Herbalists have strong herbs to do this job, but your kitchen cupboard has excellent anti-fungals such as cinnamon, thyme, oregano and garlic. I suggest that the garlic is eaten raw – one clove of garlic morning and evening. (Please be aware that a clove of garlic is not the entire head of garlic but only one of the segments.) Garlic can make you feel a bit queasy, so I recommend that you mash it with avocado pear and eat this on rye toast. Or rub it onto rye toast, then add slices of raw tomato, and drizzle olive oil on top for a delicious breakfast. In the evening, you might like it crushed into lemon juice and olive oil as a salad dressing, or crushed into mashed potato, or spread over the top of a cooked steak. You can be inventive with garlic – just try to eat it raw. Don't continue with garlic for more than a week without changing to something else, because it is a bit rough on the gut lining, and if you feel that it burns your stomach, stop immediately.

You can enjoy cinnamon tea, which is simply ½ tsp of cinnamon powder in a cup of boiling water. This is a lovely tea if you feel a bit queasy, and of course, it is a very good anti-fungal tea too.

Probiotics and pre-biotics
Within our gut lives trillions of friendly bacteria, and their job is to crowd out the unfriendly bacteria and to keep the yeast population under control. They also synthesize certain vitamins like B12, and they are also responsible for the metabolism of hormones, oestrogens in particular. Another important job is to maintain the integrity of the gut wall – in other words, to keep the intestinal wall in good order. When we take anti-biotics, these kill the friendly bacteria. The contraceptive Pill has a negative influence over the friendly bacteria, as does chlorinated water, and a poor diet. The community of bacteria that colonise our intestines may shift depending on the makeup of our overall diet.

Cherish your gut bugs
If you feel gassy and bloated, you may have too few friendly bacteria in your intestine, and there are ways of introducing friendly bacteria through your diet; although if your flora and fauna are very depleted, then you might need to take a high strength probiotic supplement. Probiotics are widely available on the market, and it is very important that you buy yours from a reputable company. I like to buy mine from a laboratory which only makes probiotics, as their entire focus and reputation rests on the quality of their bacteria.

Friendly bacteria are found in live or bio yoghurts, and I always recommend using plain live yoghurt, because the flavoured yoghurts have quite a bit of sugar in them. The little pots of probiotic drinks also tend to be very high in sugar, and this will encourage rather than deter yeast over-growth.

You can also enhance your flora and fauna population through eating fermented foods such as Kefir. Most Kefir will contain 5 strains of bacteria and two strains of healthy yeast. These bacterial cultures colonize in the intestines, retaining the probiotic benefit. Pickled fermentations of vegetables such as cabbage, cucumbers, eggplant, carrots, onions, turnips and squash also introduce friendly bacteria to the gut, as does fermented soy called Natto.

Bear in mind that bacteria are little animals, and so they need to be fed. The food they eat is called a pre-biotic or fructooligosaccharides (FOS). Foods which are rich in pre-biotics include slippery elm, onions, asparagus, Jerusalem artichokes, garlic, fruits, vegetables, legumes and grains. However, be aware that these foods can make one quite gassy too initially, so introduce them slowly.

Avoid sugary and processed foods, which feed the yeast and damage friendly bacteria. Maintaining a diet high in processed foods while taking a probiotic supplement to counteract the effects will not work. For a healthy gut and digestive system, put junk food in the bin, not in your body!

Finally, *Saccharomyces boulardii* is a yeast probiotic which helps to kill Candida, and flush other unfriendly bacteria out of the gut by preventing them from adhering to the gut wall. Even though it is a yeast, it is a friendly yeast, and also works quite compatibly with the friendly bacteria.

Using the friendly bacteria and yeast, along with avoiding sugar, eating healthy foods and drinking cinnamon tea is an effective and a safe option for helping to redress the balance of flora and fauna within your gut. By restoring the friendly bacterial balance, you will crowd out the unfriendly bacteria and yeast which cause the bloating, flatulence, bowel toxins and the symptoms associated with those. The friendly bacteria can then start to repair the gut wall and your immune system, rebuilding your health from a strong foundation.

Healing the leaky gut

Foods which inflame the gut, yeast over-growth, low levels of hydrochloric acid and other reasons can result in the gut lining becoming inflamed and perforated with holes, thus becoming 'leaky'. As a result, undigested food particles escape into the blood stream, setting up immune responses, which can cause significant health problems like recurrent headaches, constant sinus congestion and joint pains.

To diagnose a leaky gut with absolute conviction, it is necessary to perform a gut permeability test; however, as a rule of thumb you can consider that if you have discovered you have a Candida over-growth, then it is probable that you have a leaky gut. If you have food intolerances, then you will have a leaky gut, and if you have had irritable bowel syndrome or a disturbed digestive system for some years, then the likelihood of you having a leaky gut is quite high – only to be confirmed with a laboratory test.

However, there are foods, herbs and nutritional supplements which can heal the leaky gut, and eating these foods and drinking these safe and innocuous herbal teas will not do anything but good for your digestion.

Chamomile, calendula flowers and Liquorice root are herbs with a well known tradition of use to heal inflamed and leaky guts. When treating the gut, I find that teas are the most gentle and helpful as they wash over the inflamed tissues without the aggressiveness of the alcohol in tinctures. You should be able to buy these herbs easily from a health shop or herbal apothecary to make into a healing tea. Do be aware that Liquorice can raise the blood pressure and loosen the bowels.

Aloe vera juice or the African *Aloe ferox* juice both have strong traditional reputations for healing an inflamed and painful gut. Both provide the gut with healing compounds in food-state form which makes them easily acceptable and digestible to the gut, whilst at the same time they are soothing and anti-inflammatory to the intestinal lining. Aloe also provides pre-biotics, supporting the probiotic population, as well as providing soft cellulose which encourages regular and cleansing bowel movements.

Cabbage water is an old wives remedy for gut problems and we seem to like science to remind us of the wisdom of those old ladies. Nowadays we can buy posh vitamin U supplements, but in the olden days, the wives would drink the water in which cabbage had been boiled to heal ulcers and inflammations of the gut. This water is rich in vitamin U, and the cabbage itself is delicious, cheap and nourishing.

The good bacteria in the gut use the fibre from foods such as fruits, vegetables, legumes and grains to make a short-chain fatty acid called butyrate. Butyrate is an important source of energy for the cells lining the colon. This helps to keep the lining in the gut strong and healthy, especially important where leaky gut is present. It may be necessary to use L-Glutamine to 'zip' up the leaky gut. It is best to take this first thing in the morning on an empty stomach and in between meals. Allow thirty minutes before starting a meal once you have taken the L-Glutamine.

There are other options too, and your nutritionist or medical herbalist will advise you if you need stronger natural medicines.

Have a Food Intolerance test

Although this is slightly diverting from our subject of stress, it really makes a great deal of sense that if you have developed a leaky gut as a result of your stressful lifestyle, then it is highly likely that you will have food intolerances.

These intolerances are caused by your immune system setting up a negative reaction to certain foods as a result of a leaky gut. Consequently each time you eat this food, the immune system is compelled to attack it. This can leave you vulnerable to developing further problems as a result of this unnatural immune response, and also it is a burden on your body which your immune system will be grateful to be relieved of.

These tests cost a fair amount, but are well worth it because you really cannot possibly guess which foods you may have become intolerant to. You might discover that you are fine with trout, but intolerant to salmon; fine with almonds but not with hazelnuts; fine with cow's milk but intolerant to rice milk. It is well worth spending the money, and even if your test results show that you have no intolerances, that is still an answer, and a valuable answer. You can tick food intolerances off your list.

Chapter Thirteen

Rebalance the Immune System

By now it will be quite clear that stress has a profound impact on the adrenal glands, forcing them to release higher levels of cortisol than is natural, as the body attempts to survive the perceived threats. Over time, the elevated cortisol levels have a negative impact on our immune system, depressing the anti-viral and anti-bacterial arm of the immune system (Th1), whilst at the same time raising the allergic inflammatory arm of the immune system (Th2). This leads to increased vulnerability to viral infections, reduced ability to recover from these infections, and more allergic-type conditions.

The job now is to restore optimal immune balance, by decreasing inflammation whilst at the same time, raising resistance against bacteria, viruses and fungi. For those who are suffering from a post-viral syndrome or who are unable to recover from common colds or flu, the criteria is to provide the body with immune boosting herbs whilst at the same time reducing the viral load. Or, if the person is also suffering from a Candida overgrowth, then it will be necessary to reduce the fungal load by including anti-fungal agents. For those suffering from frequent colds or sometimes no colds ever, but lots of allergic symptoms, it is necessary to rebalance (or modulate) the immune system.

• Restore optimal immune function
• Reduce the viral load
• Reduce the fungal load

Typical case history

Imagine a man whose immune system has become depressed by the chronically elevated cortisol levels caused by ongoing stress. He inhales millions of bacteria and viruses with every breath, but his immune resistance is weakened and much less effective at disposing of them. Thus this on-going ineffective fight further exhausts his immune system. You can think of it like the wheels of a car spinning around in mud – working very hard, sinking deeper and not getting anywhere.

Now, imagine that our man is feeling so very burnt out that he uses high sugar foods and coffee to give him the energy that he needs to get through his demanding day. He has had several colds this year, and been prescribed courses of antibiotics which have had no effect on the viruses at all. The antibiotics did kill the infectious bacteria, but also wiped out his friendly gut bacteria, which compete with the small yeast population living in his gut, keeping it from over-growing. Because his immune system is so weak, he catches another cold pretty soon after finishing his last prescription of antibiotics.

As a result of his weakened immune system, his high sugar intake and lack of friendly bacteria in the gut – the yeast is encouraged to grow and multiply at a ferocious rate. He remains unaware of the danger which he is in, except for a feeling of uncomfortable bloating, flatulence and brain fogginess. In time, the yeast develops root-like mycelia which penetrate the gut wall, entering his blood stream, thus overloading his immune system even further. The yeast can now spread to other parts of his body. Undigested food particles slip through the permeable gaps in his gut wall, providing the white blood cells with "enemies" to deal with. His immune system becomes overwhelmed and even less effective.

What can be done?

* Stop eating sugar which feeds the yeast.
* Keep the blood sugar levels even.
* Kill the excess yeast.
* Re-populate the gut with probiotics.

- Use herbs and nutrition to heal the gut permeability.
- Reduce his viral load.
- Calm his nerves and help his sleep.
- Support his adrenal glands.
- Rebalance and boost his immune system.

Killing the invading yeast

Within the body of the yeast is a certain amount of toxic material. When the yeast dies, their structures breakdown and the toxic matter is released into the blood stream, which can make people feel very unwell, because it literally releases the poisons into the blood. This is referred to as "die-off" or the "Herxheimer reaction" and it is simplest to explain that the symptoms are very similar to a rotten hang-over.

With this in mind, I prefer to start by supporting liver function, by including in the herbal treatment prescription some milk thistle or dandelion root at the very least. It is also very important to make sure that the bowel is voiding fully with each bowel movement because if the toxins are not eliminated via the faeces, they will be re-absorbed into the blood stream again, which will increase the feelings of toxicity. This was discussed in the previous chapter.

Now you can start by killing the yeast off slowly, so that your liver is able to cope with the toxic load a little at a time. First, it is very helpful to starve the yeast by not eating anything sugary. This means avoiding completely all sweets, chocolates, hot chocolate, biscuits, cakes, honey etc. At first you may feel desperate for sugar, but if you keep your blood sugar levels even, you will find this phase is not as bad as you imagine. (See chapter 9 on blood sugar balance) If you are not hungry, your sugar cravings will be very much milder and soon forgotten. Focus instead on nourishing your body with lovely health forming foods. Slowly the yeast will begin to die, and after 2 – 3 weeks, you can move onto phase 2 where you begin actively killing the yeast with garlic and cinnamon.

There are much stronger natural anti-fungal options available, but as usual, I strongly suggest that you see a professional herbalist or nutritionist to guide you through the anti-candida process because it is a complicated process and one which must be dealt with by someone who is experienced and competent.

Probiotics

Believe it or not, the lining of our gut provides a very important and vast section of our immune system. Even more amazing is that within our gut reside more friendly bacteria than cells in our bodies. Four kilograms of our body weight is made up of gut flora and fauna. These friendly bacteria coat every corner of the small and large intestine, and one of their jobs is to actively program the intestinal immune response. Antibiotics kill these friendly bacteria, and this has a detrimental effect on our immune system. Unfortunately the space that is left by the friendly bacteria is quickly occupied by yeasts and more unfriendly bacteria; therefore, it is strongly advisable to take a course of very good quality probiotics. These will help to repopulate the gut with the correct flora, which push out the unhealthy bacteria and the yeasts. Probiotics also help to balance out the Th1 and Th2 parts of the immune system.

A very interesting probiotic is *Saccharomyces boulardii*, which itself is a yeast, but it actually destroys the Candida yeast by excreting certain fatty acids, which both kill Candida and prevent it from adhering to the gut wall. Thus it helps to flush out the Candida via the bowels, and then very elegantly, it dies itself. But *Saccharomyces boulardii* does more than just kill unfriendly gut flora – it also boosts our immune system. So this amazing yeast kills off unfriendly bacteria and yeasts, whilst at the same time stimulating our immune system, thus significantly helping to bring about balance and health. Then it dies and passes out of our bowels.

Reducing the viral load

Sambucus nigra fructus (Elderberries): Elderberries are abundant, free and fabulous anti-viral medicines to be found in any hedgerow. These berries have been used for millennia to reduce viral illnesses, and have been shown to be extremely effective against the Epstein Barr virus, Herpes virus and Influenza viruses [1]. Although there are some very good elderberry brands available, there is no reason why you cannot collect your own berries – making sure, of course that they are definitely elderberries, and make your own medicine. The berries can be collected and frozen, then whizzed into a smoothie with rice milk and a banana, or cooked into a cordial and taken each evening with hot water. Elderberries not only inhibit the virus, but they are immune tonics too, and this is an extremely safe herb to self-prescribe.

Hypericum perforatum (St John's Wort): St John's Wort is well known as having anti-depressant actions, but it is less well known for its significant anti-viral properties [2, 3, 4, 5]. In many ways, this is a perfect herb for those with post-viral fatigue or burn-out. Long ago when I studied to be a herbalist, we were taught that SJW is not an anti-depressant, but rather a nerve restorative, calming the nerves and helping to re-nourish a debilitated nervous system. By helping to restore the exhausted nervous system whilst at the same time reducing the viral load, this herb offers significant help to the over stressed and burnt out individual.

Astragalus membranaceus (Astragalus): Astragalus has also demonstrated significant anti-viral effects [6, 9], but its action on the body is somewhat different to St John's Wort. Whereas St John's Wort supports the nervous system, Astragalus strengthens stamina, and studies have confirmed its effects on chronic fatigue subjects as a stamina tonic [7], as well as noting immune restorative effects [8], and a certain strengthening effect on the cardiac muscle [9]. I do not find this a quick acting herb, but its immune building and stamina tonifying effects are slow but sure.

Olea europaea (Olive leaf): Until recently, we all thought that the olive tree was a stunningly beautiful tree which lives for hundreds of years in the Mediterranean region and produces wonderful oil which helps to keep our arteries clear and our skin soft. Now, scientists are discovering that the leaf has rather remarkable properties, in that it is powerfully anti-microbial against viruses [10], as well as a wide range of bacteria, including E coli, Staphylococcus aureus, Klebsiella pneumoniae, and fungi including Candida [11]. The plant has further medical properties, such as lowering high blood pressure, reducing cholesterol, and it acts as an anti-oxidant. In our obese and stressful society, these medicinal properties are very valuable, especially when they all come wrapped up in a single plant, and we can take our medicine as a cheap and readily available herbal tea.

Rebalancing the immune system

Vitamin D: Classically, the therapeutic benefits of vitamin D have been restricted to calcium absorption and bone mineralisation, and it has been long understood that a lack of vitamin D was responsible for rickets in children, and reduced bone mass in adults, known as osteopenia and osteoporosis.

However, more recently, it is becoming clear how important this vitamin is in relation to the immune system. Studies have shown that it down-regulates certain inflammatory chemicals of the immune system, helping modulate auto-immune diseases, as it is excellent for helping balance the Th1 and Th2 arms of the immune system. But at the same time, it also stimulates the anti-microbial parts of the immune system, and so this vitamin been shown to be very effective against influenza viruses [12], diabetes, multiple sclerosis, rheumatoid arthritis, tuberculosis, and cancers of the colon, prostate gland and breast [13].

Vitamin D is found in wild oily fish, particularly cod liver oil and salmon, with much less of the vitamin found in pellet fed farmed salmon; but the major source of vitamin D is through naked skin exposure to sunlight. The optimal range for vitamin D is between 50 – 80 ng/ml, with less than 20 ng/ml being considered a deficiency. The vast majority of my patients show results lower than 12 ng/ml, which appears to be reflective of the population as a whole, because vitamin D deficiency is now considered to be a pandemic problem in the Northern Hemisphere.

In our modern society, most people work long hours in an office, with a few weeks of holiday allocated to them each year. This translates to very little time spent outdoors in the sunshine, and consequently low vitamin D levels. If we were to spend most of our time outdoors in Africa, with very little clothing covering our skin, we would absorb 24,000 IU of vitamin D daily. Supplements of 200 IU or even 2,000 IU of Vitamin D just do not provide sufficient of this very important nutrient.

According to Dr Holick of the Boston University School of Medicine, low vitamin D levels are also associated with muscle weakness and pain, and may be misdiagnosed as fibromyalgia and chronic fatigue syndrome [13]. If you find yourself vulnerable to recurrent viral infections, and suffer from an unexplained aching body, ask your health care practitioner to check your vitamin D status, and you may find it to be deficient.

Do be aware that vitamin D is a fat soluble vitamin and thus can accumulate in the body fat. Vitamin D should not be taken as a supplement without a prior vitamin D test, and then rechecking the status to ensure that the optimal level is being maintained and that you are not in danger of vitamin D toxicity. The safest and most effective way of topping up your vitamin D status is by exposing yourself to the sunlight for 10 to 20 minutes without sunscreen (depending on the thickness of your skin) 3 – 4 times a week, and a good quality cod liver oil supplement. By eating the skin of oily fish regularly you should also obtain a good level of vitamin D, as it is stored in the skin of the fish. It may be necessary to have a vitamin D supplement in order to gain the full amount needed to balance the immune system. Speak to your therapist about this.

Trametes versicolor (Coriolus): Coriolus falls into the category of medical mushrooms which have been used in traditional Chinese medicine as general tonics for immunity and stamina. There are not many studies available for these medicines, but several point do to a very special feature: that they are able to reverse the Th1 to Th2 shift. In other words, Coriolus modulates the immune system by up-regulating Th1, and down-regulating Th2 [14, 15] so that balance is restored. Further more, Coriolus shows impressive anti-viral properties against HIV and herpes viruses, as well as demonstrating liver protective properties [16].

Foods to help balance the immune system

Zinc: The depletion of zinc may result in an imbalance between Th1 and Th2 activity. Therefore include foods rich in zinc into your diet such as tahini spread, wheatgerm, roasted butternut squash and dark chocolate.

Fish Oils: Try to have oily fish such as cod, salmon, mackerel, sardines and tuna steak, at least twice a week. This will provide you with omega 3, an essential fatty acid. This will help to balance out the immune system.

Garlic: This common food is splendid at killing viruses, bacteria and fungi, and also has anti-histaminic effects. It is best included as raw as possible in the diet, perhaps in salad dressings, crushed into mashed potatoes, mashed into avocado or in a salsa. Be careful not to eat a raw clove of garlic on its own as it is very strong and can inflame the stomach lining. Rather mash it into food.

Chapter Fourteen

Re-invigorating cellular energy

One of the commonest complaints a doctor will hear from his patients is that they are experiencing unexplained fatigue. They might not feel unwell, just inexplicably weary, lethargic, fatigued, unreasonably tired. People with chronic fatigue syndrome experience this in the extreme where they can take hours or days to recover from energy output.

It is always hardest for someone who feels so very exhausted all the time to be told that *"there is nothing wrong with you"*. You know there is something wrong with you and yet there is no confirmation, no evidence, and it is easy to wonder if you are just imagining it. Even worse, is that your family and friends might start to look at you askance, and even tell you to pull up your socks – *"Everyone gets tired at some stage"*. But this is a different tiredness. It is a tiredness which does not recover after a weekend of sleeping. It is a deep bone aching tiredness.

There are many reasons for fatigue, such as low thyroid function, menopausal symptoms, low grade chronic infection, mercury toxicity, cardiac disease, certain medications, insomnia, food intolerance or allergies, chronic inflammatory pain, gut dysbiosis, adrenal fatigue, depression and poor nutrition, to name only a few. In order to get to the bottom of the underlying problem, all of these and more need to be evaluated fully by an experienced health care practitioner, to give you the best chance of making a full health recovery. Much of the information can be gleaned through a thorough discussion whilst taking the case history, and then specific questions can be confirmed through laboratory tests.

The focus of this book is on the role that stress has on our health and lives; thus it is beyond the scope of this book to discuss all the causes and possible treatment strategies for other causes of fatigue. However, human beings are complex and there are quite likely several causes for our patient's feelings of debilitating fatigue, which may include one or more of the above reasons as well as stress. As I have outlined earlier – one body-system out of balance will impact on another system, and so the underlying cause, as well as the presenting symptoms, must be considered with equal concern.

Mitochondrial damage

As you can appreciate, many causes of fatigue are hidden and not obvious. One of the most hidden causes lies deep within the cells themselves, and we are only just discovering some answers to severe fatigue deep within the cells. Our energy does not come from a particular organ in our bodies, but from tiny organelles found floating in the cellular fluid of each one of the approximately 60 trillion cells in our body. These organelles, called mitochondria, act as the energy generators for our cells and our body. They use the glucose from our food and oxygen from our breath to produce packets of energy called ATP. For several reasons this natural cycle of energy production can become dysfunctional, leaving the mitochondria struggling to produce the energy we require to live productive lives.

Within the mitochondria of each cell, runs the energy cycle called the Krebs Cycle. You might find it useful to imagine it like many cogs in a large energy-producing machine – recycling packets of energy called ATP. This gives us our cellular energy. When we are feeling good and full of energy, we know that our recycling is on top form.

In fact recycling occurs approximately every 10 seconds in a normal person, producing more than 90% of cellular energy. In cases of CFS or ME, the recycling slows and our cell has to 'hibernate', waiting until more ATP has been manufactured. The only way the body can make fresh ATP for our cells is from fresh ingredients, such as D-ribose and other vitamins and minerals.

CFS and ME sufferers have been found to have low ATP levels, as they cannot seem to re-cycle fast enough. Sometimes when the body is very short of ATP it will make some more from glucose, but this encourages lactic acid production. This lactic acid stays in the muscles, causing the typical muscle pain which ME/CFS suffers experience. People who do lots of sports or exercise also make lactic acid in their muscles but they often rid this effectively. In order to rid the lactic acid, you need the mitochondria to be functioning well.

It has been discovered that this energy production cycle can become clogged with toxins, and so the cell has to divert its energy production to another less productive cycle which can manufacture very little ATP, very slowly. This accounts for the very slow recovery time that many people with ME suffer from, after even the mildest exertion. The toxins may be due to gut fermentation, or toxic metals such as mercury, inhalation of toxic fumes, or possibly even pesticide residues from modern food production methods. This is why supporting your liver and digestive processes is so important to encourage healthy detoxification.

There is evidence now to show that the mitochondria can also become actually damaged through stress, thus making it very difficult to produce ATP, increasing lactic acid build-up in the cells, and decreasing brain function which makes cognition more foggy.

How stress makes us tired

Several studies have demonstrated that chronic ongoing stress and the stress hormone cortisol, can damage the mitochondria and their ability to produce the energy packets of ATP effectively. Here we can refer back to Dr Martin Pall's hypothesis of the nitric oxide NO/ONOO cycle briefly outlined in Chapter 7, where he explains that a likely mechanism may be that stress results in a dramatic increase in damaging free radicals. These literally tear open the membrane surrounding the mitochondria, damaging the energy producing organelles and the DNA within the mitochondria, and thus leading to great difficulty in producing energy by the cell [1,2,3,4,5]. The other ways that we increase the free radicals in our body may be due to smoking, eating foods fried in old oil, from pollution or radiation, or as a result of chronic inflammation.

Other causes of poor mitochondrial function

Vitamin or mineral deficiencies: The generation of ATP requires magnesium, vitamin B, iron, copper and zinc. These nutrients may be deficient due to poor diet, poor quality of food such as non-organic hydroponically grown foods, poor digestion, a damaged gut which cannot absorb nutrients from the food or gut parasites.

Lack of anti-oxidants: The mitochondria themselves produce free radicals. Sometimes if there are not enough anti-oxidants available to 'mop-up' these free radicals, the free radicals can damage the mitochondria.

Low thyroid function: Thyroid malfunction can also produce fatigue, this is because T3 directly boosts energy metabolism in mitochondria. Thyroid testing is therefore important.

Food allergies/intolerances causing gut fermentation: This gut fermentation produces toxins, which can clog up the mitochondria.

Healing the damaged mitochondria

First of all, if you feel that stress has got you into a position where your cells themselves are damaged, you really need to do everything you can to re-adjust your life so that you introduce areas of rest and repair into your life style. A lot of people argue that this is impossible, but before you argue – consider the consequences of not doing that.

Eureka Moment!

I, myself, remember one day crossing the road and thinking that once I get this job done and that event out of the way, that I can relax and stop racing about in this constant state of great busyness, somewhat stressfully. Half way across the road it dawned on me that there will *always* be another job to do and a lot going on in my life. What I had to do was learn how to manage my life and my mind, so that life becomes a pleasure all the time.

Dramatically increasing the cellular anti-oxidant levels will help to quench the free-radicals, thereby limiting their damaging effects on the cells and the mitochondria. It is like throwing water on the fire.

The toxins which clog up the mitochondrial cogs have to be cleared. In order to do this, you need to identify whether the toxins come from outside the body, for instance industrial fumes, paint fumes, poor dietary choices, or pesticides, or whether they come from inside the body, due to gut fermentation, Candida overgrowth, mercury fillings, poor bowel elimination etc.

The mitochondria should also be provided with the nutritional support to heal their surrounding membrane, as well as the necessary herbs, vitamins and minerals so that they can be utilized in the manufacturing of energy.

Rest and recover
Quench free radicals
Detox the cells
Nourish the cells and mitochondria

Quench free radicals with anti-oxidants

Foods rich in anti-oxidants: There are plenty of anti-oxidant products on the market, and just looking at the vast array can be incredibly confusing. There are two points to bear in mind. The best anti-oxidant regime includes a wide variety of anti-oxidant foods. We now know that taking vitamin C and E is absolutely just not enough. You can go a very long way towards increasing your anti-oxidant level with food alone.

There is so much that can be done with diet to improve one's health; and this is wonderfully empowering because it puts your health back into your own hands. For those who are terribly fatigued, this can be a moot point, because they can barely manage to go shopping for food, let alone cook a fantastic meal. Perhaps you can recruit friends and family members to rally around and help you a little, until you have restored your health to the point where you can feel enthusiastic about cooking healthy meals for yourself. Alternatively, cook in greater quantities, then divide into portions and freeze convenient meals for yourself.

With regard to diet, first of all, remember that you are focusing on keeping your blood sugar levels even, so that your energy feels more stable. Then you need to be strict about junk food, so that you are not ingesting poisons. The deep fried fast food junk food is **full** of damaging substances which increase free radical damage to the mitochondria, increase the toxic load on the cells, interfere with your hormones, and clog up the detoxification pathways of the cells and the liver. Just watch the well known film "Supersize Me" to get an idea how badly junk food will affect your health.

I have a patient who had suffered from ME and terrible pain in her legs for years. Even after the fatigue abated, her leg muscles were still painful. When we did a gentle detoxification program the pain cleared up and she telephoned me a few days ago to say that this was the first holiday in years when she was able to go out and do things every day without having to take a rest day in between.

There are so many gloriously health promoting foods to be enjoyed instead.

Let food be your medicine

The Rainbow Diet
Rainbow Diet incorporates all the different colours of vegetables into your diet: red, orange, yellow, green, blue, indigo and violet. Foods with a variety of colours have different healthy nutrients: vitamins, minerals, microelements and are bursting with anti-oxidants. Spinach, red, yellow and green peppers, asparagus, cranberries, blackberries, red currants, raspberries, red grapes, lemons, grapefruit, beetroot, buckwheat, fresh rosemary, fresh thyme, fresh basil, fresh peppermint, dark chocolate, red wine, citrus juice, olive oil, alfalfa and bean sprouts

Herbs with anti-oxidant actions
Curcuma longa (Turmeric): Turmeric is one of those wonder spices that scientists are becoming very excited about, particularly in relation to cancer cells. Turmeric exerts significant anti-oxidant effects on cells [6, 7], and one study showed how it increases ATP in cells (the energy packages produced by the mitochondria) where

they had previously been depleted [7]. Herbalists use this spice for its profound anti-oxidant effects, anti-inflammatory effects, and also because it is a liver supporting herb, which is very important when we initiate a detoxification program.

When you use herbs to start removing the toxic build up in cells, those toxins are washed into the blood stream and from there, taken to the liver. It is the job of the liver to "process" the toxins and flush them into the bowel for elimination. However if the liver is already clogged with toxic accumulations, the extra toxins overload the liver, resulting in a back up of toxins in the blood stream. The consequence of that is that the person feels much worse, rather than better, and it is actually dangerous to have these toxins floating about freely. Therefore it is of the utmost importance when detoxifying the body that the bowel contents should be moving easily, and that the liver is being well supported by herbs which encourage the flushing of bile from the liver into the bowel. In this way, the toxic accumulations are washed out with the bile into the bowel for prompt elimination.

Turmeric works by mopping up the free radicals which damage the mitochondria [8], calming inflammation, and also by acting as a liver tonic – encouraging the flushing of bile into the bowel. Bear in mind that unrelenting stress results in fatigued adrenal glands which cannot produce enough cortisol, our own natural anti-inflammatory hormone. I have often found that turmeric can significantly help to ease the painful muscles of people with long term debilitating fatigue, until the adrenal glands recover.

Schisandra chinensis (Schizandra): Schizandra is a sour tasting berry which can be tremendously helpful in treating severe debilitating fatigue caused by stress. It is a classic adaptogenic herb, effectively helping the body to cope well with stress by reducing cortisol and the effects of stress on the body 9. Schizandra is also a potent liver-supporting herb, encouraging the detoxification process and helping to quench free radicals [10, 11]; but at the same time, it increases stamina and reduces fatigue because it protects the mitochondria against free radical damage. For those who feel very hot, I find this to be a cooling and refreshing herb, and just as an aside, I find it very helpful for women who are experiencing menopausal flushes and at the same time feel completely wrung out.

Rosmarinus officinalis (Rosemary): Rosemary is a very common garden plant and well established as a traditional remedy for improving circulation, gladdening the heart and relieving pain. Indeed, if you rub your hand over the plant, the fragrance which floats towards your nose is so beautiful that it does indeed gladden the heart.

For our discussion, it is worth noting that rosemary has significant anti-oxidant properties, quenching the free radicals in the mitochondria [12], thus protecting your energy factories against damage. It also protects the liver [13] and thus supports the detoxification process which is necessary to unclog the mitochondria from harmful toxic debris.

Rosemary is perhaps best known for its ability to improve circulation and memory. This seems to be achieved by its ability to mildly thin the blood and thereby facilitate the smooth flow of blood through tiny capillaries. It will also improve circulation through its significant anti-spasmodic action on the blood vessels. By relaxing the blood vessels, blood can flow more easily and deliver the valuable nutrients to the cells whilst at the same time, removing the toxins from the cells, taking them to be processed in the liver. This herb also relaxes muscles – one of the reasons why the herb has been traditionally used to relieve muscle pain [14, 15, 16].

Zingiber officinalis (Ginger): Plain old ginger root is an absolutely marvellous circulatory stimulant and anti-inflammatory herb. As

145

a result it is very helpful in relieving cold and painful muscles [17]. Furthermore, it has anti-oxidant, anti-viral and liver supporting properties amongst its many other health benefits [18, 19]. Best of all, it is readily available and with its delicious taste and comforting effect on the body, this herb can be used at home to bring a lot of relief to debilitated people. It is also helpful for those who feel "cold in the gut" and their digestive system has shut down. When people are too tired, they are actually too tired to digest their food, and ginger helps to wake up the digestive system.

Ginger and Rosemary tea

This is a warming and joyful tea with anti-oxidant, liver supporting, anti-microbial and circulatory stimulating properties. More than that, it is delicious and very comforting. I like it particularly for those who are so debilitated, that they do not even have the energy to digest their food. This tea warms the stomach and helps to support digestion.

It is so simple. Just add a sprig of rosemary to a cup of boiling water, with 5 slices of fresh ginger root. Then add a slice of lemon and a little honey to taste. Drink this tea two to three times a day to support your liver, improve your memory, relax your mind, lift your spirits and ease muscle pains.

Supplements which help to repair the mitochondria

NT Factor (Lipid replacement therapy) – this particular supplement contains glycophospholipids, which help repair the damaged mitochondrial membrane by providing the building blocks of phospholipids and other lipids, along with anti-oxidants, vitamins and minerals needed for the mitochondria. Do not be confused – this is not an essential fatty acid, it is different from the omega 3, 6 and 9's, and I have seen very positive results in people using this supplement.

Other supplements such as Acetyl-l-Carnitine, Co Q10,

D-Ribose, Magnesium and B12 help towards restoring the normal functioning of the mitochondria. Vitamins and minerals which are required by the mitochondria or cell for energy production include magnesium, B vitamins, copper, iron and zinc.

Pace yourself
Have rest days
Allow the mitochondria to recover!

Herbs which restore energy

Miraculously there are plants which can restore energy to the exhausted and fatigued body, but I must make a very strong note of caution here. They should never be used without taking into account all the surrounding points which I have made about stress and fatigue. One absolutely cannot continue to flog the proverbial dead (or nearly dead) horse without it eventually collapsing – no matter how much ginseng you feed it.

Adaptogenic herbs are absolutely marvellous when used correctly, but should also be used with great care. With this in mind, they are only mentioned here for information purposes, as this book cannot take the place of a professional medical herbalist's detailed assessment of your health state, and the careful attention to prescribing a herbal formulae uniquely fitted to you.

The adaptogenic herbs

The herbs which support energy are generally classed as adaptogens. This is a fairly loosely defined term, but essentially it refers to a plant which helps us cope or adapt to stressful situations. In other words, these plants support our survival during difficult periods of life. A good example is the Siberian ginseng *(Eleutherococcus senticosus)*, which was discussed in chapter 11. The root of this plant was used by the elderly peasants in Russia to help them survive long and freezing winters with little food. Another example is *Sutherlandia frutescens* which the Zulus of South Africa call "insiswa", meaning "to take away the darkness". This beautiful plant with red bubble-like flowers was taken by the Zulu warriors after their wars when they returned exhausted and suffering from depression, or post-traumatic stress disorder, as we now know that soldiers often do.

In both of these examples, the plants helped men and women to cope and survive through either the stressful situation itself, or the effects that the stress had on the person's well-being. Our lives may not be as dramatic as either of these examples, but in many cases, the stress is long term and unrelenting. Our bodies cannot differentiate between what *type* of stress we are experiencing – just that we *are* experiencing stress and after some time the body has difficulty coping. This is when we need adaptogenic herbs, as well as the adrenal supporting herbs, calming herbs, excellent food, proper rest and kindness to ourselves.

Adaptogens seem to support the physical endurance of those under stress by supplying micro-nutrients to the cells, as well as keeping nitric oxide (NO) and cortisol hormone at a normal level and thus protecting the ATP energy generating molecules. They reduce the damage caused by free radicals, whilst at the same time supporting the adrenal glands.

Several of the adaptogenic herbs have already been discussed under different chapters.

Withania somnifera – discussed in chapter 11
Rhodiola rosea – discussed in chapter 11
Astragalus membranaceus – chapter 12
Coriolus (Trametes) versicolor – chapter 12
Dioscorea villosa – is very briefly touched on in chapter 15
Schisandra chinensis – is discussed above.

Codonopsis pilosula

Codonopsis is sometimes referred to as poor man's ginseng, as it is cheaper than Panax ginseng, and the effect is milder. I find this herb absolutely fabulous. It is not a stimulating herb, but quietly builds strength and stamina in the body of the person under strain, whilst at the same time providing support for cognitive function. So often, I hear people with CFS/ME telling me that they feel low in mood. Well, of course they feel low – so would anyone who feels ill all the time, exhausted all the time and usually suffering with constant body pains. But they are not ill because they are depressed, they feel low because they are ill and not getting any better. When people start to take Codonopsis, along with a protocol designed specifically for them, they start to feel better – their mood improves.

Sutherlandia frutescens (Sutherlandia)

Sutherlandia or Cancer bush has been referred to as the African adaptogen par excellence, and it has a very strong tradition as a herb to take during chronic stress. Sutherlandia is an amazing herb, which has an immune stimulating effect, reducing high blood sugar levels, relieving depression, killing cancer cells, building stamina; but for now we are focusing on its influence on the adrenal glands and the effects of stress.

Two studies in South Africa showed that Sutherlandia maintained low cortisol levels during periods of stress, that way protecting the body from the ravages of free radicals and the other negative effects that long term stress and elevated cortisol levels can produce. The herb also prevented the breakdown of progesterone to cortisol [20, 21], thereby sparing the "progesterone steal" process which we discussed earlier in the book (Chapter 6) relating to stress and infertility.

Like so many of the cellular restorative herbs we have looked at, Sutherlandia shows anti-oxidant actions, which may also account for its traditional anti-inflammatory [22] and strengthening applications. It is rich in a compound called L-canavanine which has anti-viral properties, and we see this effect reflected in its traditional use in Africa against HIV and the influenza virus. Another important constituent of Sutherlandia is the relaxing and anti-convulsive amino acid called GABA [23]. Again, scientific evidence supports the traditional use of the plant as an anti-epileptic herb, and in particular, its profound ability to relieve anxiety, depression and stress.

All these actions together suggest that Sutherlandia could be an almost perfect herb to use in stress related illness in that it calms the mind, reduces the elevated blood sugar levels, reduces free radical attack on the cells, supports the stamina and the immune system and kills off rogue viruses.

Centella asiatica (Gotu Kola)
Centella is a quiet herb, and one which I have valued for years, helping those who are burnt out, by gently restoring brain function. When people burn out they can feel foggy in the brain and can have great difficulty holding a conversation, reading or even following a television story. Sometimes this symptom is so severe that the person will describe it as "brain ache" and may have a strong aversion to any sensory stimulation, often wishing to remain in a quiet and darkened room. Centella helps to restore normal brain function and has been used by the healers of India for this purpose for about 2000 years. When discussing Withania (Ashwaghanda) (in Chapter 11), I briefly mentioned the Ayurvedic Rasayanas, which are adaptogenic herbs, but this class is further divided into Medhya Rasayanas, which are specifically brain restorative herbs, or "wisdom herbs".

Modern science and ancient tradition agree that Centella delays ageing in the brain, improves mood and cognition, helps regeneration of nerves in the brain, and has memory enhancing effects [24] – so much so, that it is currently being investigated for Alzheimer's disease [25]. As we have seen so many times with the other adaptogenic herbs, there are anti-oxidant actions, but, with this herb, specifically in the tissues of the brain.

Cordyceps sinensis

Now this is a truly fascinating mushroom. High on the Tibetan plateau at about 3000m lives a certain species of caterpillar which becomes infected by a fungus. This fungus then proceeds to feed off and eventually kill the caterpillar, so that what is left is a thin brown reed-like fungus growing out of the head of a mummified caterpillar. 1500 years ago the Tibetan herdsmen noticed that their animals became much stronger and more fortified when eating this fungus, and so the word spread to local doctors and it became so highly regarded, that collecting it was known as the fungal gold rush. Happily for us, these days Cordyceps is no longer grown on caterpillar heads, but in a laboratory making it much more available, affordable and just as effective [26].

Cordyceps has two major traditional properties. The first is its anti-ageing actions and ability to enhance athletic performance, and the second is that it improves low libido and increases fertility in both men and women. So you can imagine why it was so highly in demand. It is also acknowledged as an anti-viral agent and immune modulator, which makes Cordyceps highly valuable for those with debilitating post viral fatigue.

Modern science confirms these ancient observations by noting its ability to increase exercise endurance as well as quell free radical damage [27]. Other studies demonstrate that it enhances the immune system, increases the ability of the mitochondria to generate ATP, and increases the natural manufacturing of testosterone [28]. All of these actions will not only increase strength, immunity and stamina but also a person's sense of well-being.

Chapter Fifteen

Rebalancing the hormones

This is not a subject which I am going to elaborate on very much. It is so important that if your thyroid gland is under-performing or you are oestrogen dominant, or low in testosterone, that these issues are addressed very carefully by a qualified health care professional, and always according to your unique needs.

As you have read in Part 1, the effect of too much on-going stress can often have an unrecognised and negative influence on the hormones. The adrenal glands are so closely linked to hormonal health, that if the adrenals are out of kilter, the other hormones are likely to be too. Bear in mind how too much cortisol reduces thyroid function. Consider how the under-production of cortisol from the exhausted adrenal glands can result in the "progesterone steal" from the ovaries, thus swinging the female hormones into oestrogen dominance. This is especially relevant these days when women are competing in the work place, and still trying to run a home and conceive. So many times, I have found that when we run adrenal, and female hormone tests, the adrenal glands are struggling and the progesterone is too low to support a pregnancy.

It is of utmost importance that you concentrate on restoring your overall health, which will have the knock-on effect of bringing your hormones back into balance.

Natural Progesterone
Natural progesterone cream is available on the internet, but the word "natural" is somewhat misleading. Both natural progesterone cream and Wild Yam cream have been meddled with to produce

a steroid structure which mimics progesterone. Natural Wild Yam is not a supplement for progesterone, but the herb is actually a very good adrenal and hormone balancing tonic, and it is a plant which I find very supportive in these cases. Do be aware that if you decide to self-prescribe, as is the way many people choose to go nowadays, that by applying progesterone crème to your body, you are simply topping up that hormone often at a very high dose, but the underlying cause or imbalance remains unaddressed. Addressing the underlying imbalance and cause of this imbalance is ALWAYS the focus in holistic medicine. You cannot hope to become healthy by simply pushing the imbalance in the other direction and think that everything will be fine now. It will not. Ill health is always about imbalance, and restoring the optimal balance is the key to regaining optimal health.

Ill health is alwasys about imbalance.
Restoring optimal homeostatic balance is the key to regaining vibrant health.

This is why I urge you again and again in this book to bring the balance back into your life style, eat a balanced diet, think balanced thoughts, use a balanced treatment program. **Rebalance, Rebalance, Rebalance.** Then your body will default back to its original blue-print of vibrant health again.

PART THREE

Staying Well – Living Well

Chapter Sixteen

Staying Well

It is all about balance
It has become clear numerous times in this book, that maintaining optimal health depends on balance. Stress pushes our cortisol up. Cortisol pushes our immune system down and our blood sugars up. Stress and cortisol disrupt our sex hormones, our mood and our gut flora balance. The knock-on effect of one imbalance creates the next imbalance, and so it goes on with a domino effect. It has always been understood that it is the homeostatic balance within and around our cells which determines our health and feeling of well-being.

Less understood is how to exert a positive influence over this homeostatic balance in order to restore and maintain our good health. Meditation appears to have an excellent role to play here. Herbal medicine, nutritional medicine, and other healing modalities can help to restore the homeostatic balance and health as you have seen in previous chapters, but once you feel better again, no doubt you will urgently want to avoid feeling that unwell again.

We have seen how stress significantly disrupts the homeostatic balance and so it is not difficult to conclude that within the daily running of our lives, maintaining good health must have something to do with maintaining a *sense* of balance.

Our work vs home life balance, our mental/spiritual/emotional balance, our need to earn versus our need to be creative and play, our body's requirement for exercise vs rest. All these poles require balancing in order for us to live a full life with sustainable energy.

So many people have said to me that all they want is to get their lives back so that they can get on with living the way they used to. But it doesn't work that way, I am afraid. It really is all very well taking the supplements and herbs as described in Part 2, but once you have "got your life back" – are you going to go right back to living it the way you did before you became unwell? If you do make that choice it is highly likely that you will become ill again, because you will be inflicting the same damage on a pre-weakened body. With that sort of pressure, your health will quite likely give way again.

"Me Time"

I feel that the abbreviation for Myalgic Encephalomyelitis "M.E." is actually very relevant. As I have pointed out before, my experience in treating scores of people with ME has taught me that many of these people have usually spent a life time of running around achieving, trying to be perfect, looking after others, or have had tremendous family stress imposed upon them, and generally being very busy. They have for the most part, completely ignored their own selves, and so I find it a wonderful irony that the illness which can be caused by all this busyness is called ME. It is time to think about Me.

M.E. is a MAJOR wake-up call from your body saying: *"If you will not stop and take note of what I need, then I will make you stop by becoming so exhausted that you have to stop"*.

This is the time when you have to learn to honour yourself. You need "Me Time". I assure you that this is the absolute crux upon which your recovery and continued health depends.

Me Time means:

- Taking the time to eat properly.
- Doing the things that you love to do.
- Having some quiet time where you may read, play your guitar, write poetry, paint, knit, plant your carrots, watch the clouds, pray to your God or Goddess, meditate, spend time in nature.
- Quietly reconnecting with yourself and who you really are.
- Resting gently.
- Going to bed early enough.

Me Time also means having fun, expressing your creativity or who you really are:

- Riding your motor bike
- Making chutney or hedgerow wine
- Going to a comedy club with your friends
- Playing a make-believe game with your children
- Sewing a flamboyant coat of many colours
- Writing a novel
- Learning to ice skate
- Baking a cake
- Going sailing
- Camping in a yurt in the forest

Make a list of the things that you would love to do, and choose the gentler option for now. We may live in a wealthy world, but it is not a very gentle world. Choose the gentler option for yourself. If you still have plenty of stamina but you feel yourself falling – then choose the more lively options. Do what it is that makes your heart sing.

You cannot protect yourself and thrive at the same time

Professor of biology, Bruce Lipton [1] studied the behaviour of human endothelial cells in laboratory glass dishes and noted that when nutrition was introduced to the dish of live cells, the cells gravitated towards the nutrients which allowed them to grow and thrive. Not terribly surprisingly, when a poisonous substance was introduced to the live cells, the cells moved away. He noticed something much more interesting however. In order to protect themselves from harm, the cells also shut down all the portals to their exterior environment so as to wall themselves off from the toxins. They turned themselves into miniature isolated protected citadels. In his book The Biology of Belief, Lipton makes a very relevant connection. The cells were not able to concurrently *grow* and protect themselves at the same time.

In order to grow, they needed to open the channels of communication with their external environment, so as to allow the ingestion of nutrients and the excretion of waste. In order to protect themselves from the toxic environment, they had to move away and close all channels to the external environment. Thus they could either protect themselves, or grow, but could not do both at the same time. This, he noted is very similar to human behaviour in that you cannot protect yourself and thrive at the same time. You can protect yourself and survive for a while, but you can't thrive in such an environment.

In our human situation and in the social context within which we live, we cannot expect to thrive when we constantly have to protect ourselves from a poisonous environment. Humans, animals and plants only grow and thrive in an environment which is caring and nutritious, and we wither or parts of us die when we live on junk food and with unkindness.

Sometimes people drag us down or we work ridiculously long hours, choose to drink alcohol to calm down, home life may be confrontational, certain family members might be far too demanding. These situations vampire our energy and throw our lives out of balance. Our relationship with toxic situations is not conducive to radiant health and energy. Sometimes these situations or relationships can be healed or revised, and sometimes we need to move away from them.

Do consider your own life, whether there are any environments, situations, people, dietary choices, or habits which are metaphorically or literally poisonous to you? You might react to them by feeling that you dread facing them, or inwardly cringe away from them. Perhaps you feel tired at the thought of being in this situation, or an inner sense of rage. Do you feel that you might be healthier if you moved away from this environment and towards a more wholesome one?

Follow your own path

It is generally well accepted that research into the psychology of those suffering with Chronic Fatigue Syndrome shows a trend towards those who are high achievers, or those who have undergone prolonged and unacknowledged stress.

Years ago when I worked on my MSc dissertation, I wanted to understand why people suffering from M.E. were so frequently high achievers. These people try 110% hard at work or at home, they tend to be people-pleasers, and the "work hard-play hard" type. When I discussed this with my sample group of those who had suffered and recovered from M.E., they consistently revealed to me that through most of their lives they had suppressed their own needs or dreams, rather following the expectations of others. These people did this to gain acceptance or to feel safe and lovable. It didn't matter whether their mother actually had other expectations of her child; it was simply enough that the child believed she needed to achieve or behave in a certain manner in order to be loved. In not following their own paths in life, or over compensating – they became people-pleasers, perfectionists or worked too hard and ultimately burnt themselves out.

Then, I asked the same people what was the turning point in their recovery from M.E. They told me that it was when they finally learnt to accept themselves and followed their own needs. They followed their heart and focused on spending time with people who are good to be around, and by doing the work or hobbies that they were born to do, or that they love to do. In other words, they treat themselves with love by fulfilling their inner and unique creativity. By working like this, you work with joy, and the joy is energy giving and healthy.

Listen to your body

The vast majority of chronically fatigued people that I have helped have told me that one of the hardest things to get their head around is allowing themselves time to rest, or to be looked after by someone. They work so hard at looking after everyone else, and have an overwhelming fear of being thought of as lazy or not pulling their weight. As a result they run around doing all sorts of tasks – completely forget about their own needs. All this time they totally ignore their body's plea for rest.

Almost every time I have met someone with this illness, they tell me that for years they have ignored the message from their bodies, telling them that they are tired and need to rest. One woman told me how she lies in bed every night aching with fatigue, but still will not stop rushing about. I explain that they have become deaf to their own needs, and they need to re-learn how to hear and honour their inner message of *"I need to rest"*. Instead they usually ignore the message and send another one back saying *"I just have to finish this job"* or *"I don't have time to rest"*. Now I urge them to immediately obey the message. The very minute that you perceive the message from your own body saying *"I am starting to feel a little tired now"*, you must do everything you can to stop what you are doing and sit down. You need to remind yourself that it is quite possible to continue with the job in half an hour's time.

If this is too difficult, it might be easier for you to schedule into your daily routine a mid-morning rest for half an hour, a proper lunch break and a mid afternoon rest of half an hour. This is not time to look at your emails, or do the bills. This is time when you relax and enjoy your rest. Go outside and lie in the sun for a little while. This rest period will help to build your energy, and you will find that you can achieve just as much, but with less of that aching fatigue at the end of the day. It is very important that you accept this permission to rest a little while.

You may worry that others will think your house is a mess – they won't, and if they do, well so what anyway? It is your house. You are probably far more critical about your house than anyone else is. Soothe your inner perfectionist with thoughts of gentleness towards yourself rather than perpetuating the inner tyrant. Be kind to yourself. Let others be kind to you too.

Perhaps you are reading this and thinking to yourself – *"Well that is all very well, but I work and have a family to care for. I haven't got the time"*. This brings us to the next major step that you can take to help bring balance back into your life.

Let others help you

So many people I see with this illness are very independent. This may be either because they dare not ask for help, or they do not have a partner, or in most cases, because they will not allow their family and friends to help them.

Recently I asked a very busy and completely exhausted lady if she ever allows her partner to help her and she said that she does not. When I asked her how she thinks he feels about this, she suddenly burst into tears, saying that he feels pushed out. This was a very important moment for this lady, because she suddenly realised that he wants to help her. It would make him feel useful to protect and care for the woman he loves. By not allowing herself to rest and be cared for, she continues flogging the proverbial dead horse, making her partner feel redundant and powerless. Because she insists on doing it all herself, she denies him the joy of demonstrating how much he loves her.

I am not saying that you should lie on your bed and do nothing for months, although some people are so ill with exhaustion that this is all they can do. This lady will continue to work, but perhaps her partner will make supper whilst she enjoys a soothing bath, and she will allow him to fetch the kids or bring her a cup of tea on the sofa, so that she can allow her body to recover from years of self-abuse.

If you really insist that there are jobs to do which cannot be ignored, and you cannot bear to ask your family to do them, perhaps you could pay someone to do your ironing or cleaning, or discuss with your boss that you need an assistant, or to reduce your hours.

People love to help those they love, so please let your loved ones help you. Don't be afraid to ask, and don't feel guilty. It will make them feel good, develop a lovely sense of togetherness, and bring to you a warm feeling of being nurtured and cared for. This is absolutely necessary for your recovery.

Instant balance:

The most immediate and one of the most significant things you can do for your health and to restore balance is to keep your blood sugars even. Most (perhaps all?) highly stressed people have very erratic eating patterns and therefore erratic blood sugar levels. This manifests in a feeling of weakness, with very little feeling of reliable stamina. If you avoid breakfast, your blood sugars will be too low, then you have coffee and a croissant, and it swings sharply up, but the insulin kicks in, and down the blood sugars plummet again; but because you are too busy, you only notice when you are becoming irritable with tiredness, so you eat a sandwich of poor nutritional value. Up they go again, swinging up and down throughout the day. It is like walking over an earthquake. Very erratic, exhausting and unsustainable.

- Drop the caffeinated drinks
- Have a proper breakfast as discussed in Part Two
- A nourishing snack mid-morning
- A decent lunch with protein and salad or soup
- Another nutritious snack mid afternoon
- A light but wholesome supper
- And possibly a very small snack at bed time.
- Keep yourself hydrated with water or herbal teas.

By eating small quantities of highly nutritious food throughout the day you will find that immediately you feel on much more solid ground. That very day, your body will feel calmer because it is no longer panicking about swinging blood sugars and trying to cope with cortisol levels shooting up due to low blood sugar. You will be feeding your cells with nutrients that can be used to heal your body, and by not over burdening your digestive system with large stodgy meals, the gut is able to easily digest and absorb these nutrients. In this way you are treating your body with respect – and it will pay off immediately.

The trick to maintaining this program is by being organized. Make a list of the foods that you want to eat in the week and get the food into your home so that it is readily available. You will be amazed at how much stronger, calmer and in control you feel with immediate effect. Cook in larger quantities and freeze portions so that you have a healthy ready meal waiting for you when you are too tired to cook.

Always keep some energy in the bank
More than likely until recently you were, or still are, running not only on empty, but you have drained your energy reserve tank too. This is not sustainable and cannot go on. It won't go on because

you will simply run out of energy and your health will collapse if it hasn't already done so.

Try to think of your energy as petrol in your car. If you run the petrol tank empty, the car will stop and your journey will grind to a halt. The same goes for your body. If you insist on pushing yourself too hard, your body will rebel against your mind, and your health will collapse under the strain.

Imagine a bank savings account (in the good old days when we still got interest on our money). The more money you had in the account, the more the interest built up. The same goes for your energy levels. If you guard your energy well and make sure that you always keep 20% in reserve, your long term energy and stamina levels will grow.

Some people find it hard to know when they are running low on energy. If you keep practicing, you will find that you become more attuned to your energy levels again, and you will become better at gauging when you need to take a little rest. It is just that you have lost touch with that little voice telling you that it is time to take it a bit easy now; but that voice is still there, and as you practice listening, you will start to hear it again.

Keep it in perspective

A lot of people who have had adrenal exhaustion or Chronic Fatigue Syndrome, find that they are highly sensitive to even the smallest bit of stress and become extremely agitated over tiny issues. This is quite understandable because their organism has endured too much stress and cannot take any more. The problem is that this intolerance can manifest as irritability, irrational rage or a longing to get away from it all. This can be very difficult to live with and also challenging and confusing for the person's family to live with. The vicious irony is that this excessive sensitivity to stress is very stressful in itself.

I have seen people really lose their rag over the tiniest issues, and become quite incandescent with fury. Not only do they alienate others, but this is an incredible waste of energy, and once the fury has died down, they can feel really awful about themselves, so they beat themselves up over it, which is even more of a waste of energy.

It is better to be kind to yourself and if you are feeling particularly sensitive one day, to stay away from potentially aggravating people or situations, if at all possible, until you feel better. Some people find that they need a lot of time alone with sensory deprivation to recover their ability to deal with the franticness of the world that we live in. Sensory deprivation means enjoying spending time in silence, just quietly and gently pottering about. Be aware of your blood sugar levels, making sure that they are comfortable, because low blood sugars can make one feel even more irritable.

Do try to keep some perspective and bear in mind that most people are trying to be helpful, even if sometimes they go about it in a clumsy way. Bear in mind too that most people don't understand this condition and make take offence at your snappiness. It can be very helpful to explain to your family how you are feeling, and that this is very difficult for you. Ask them to be patient with you at these times, and to give you the space and kindness that you need (obviously you won't abuse this grace).

Putting yourself first

Some people might argue that it is too selfish to think of yourself all the time and to put yourself first, but I would argue that it can be seen as being socially responsible. I am not saying that you put yourself first at the expense of others, but that you consider yourself respectfully. If you allow yourself to be put upon by other people – even if you are the personification of angelic generosity – you will eventually become fatigued and feel resentful. You might try to hide the annoyance, but one way or another it will show, and usually upon those who don't deserve to be snapped at. Shop assistants or other drivers can frequently be the victims of suppressed anger.

If you feel that a relationship is not working, do address the problem. This can be done in a kindly manner with the aim of a win-win outcome. Bringing it out into the open will relieve both of you of a heavy burden and you will both feel so much lighter and happier that the issue has finally been addressed. The same goes for if you are allowing yourself to be taken advantage of – kindly and firmly put a stop to it. Patrol your boundaries kindly.

In taking responsibility for your own sense of well being, you protect your health, you protect others from your irritable moods, you feel happier and not resentful and you teach people that it is acceptable for them to respect themselves too. Of course, you will also help others when you can, and when you do help them it is done with joy and pleasure. However, you do not help people to such a degree that you feel burnt out and resentful – that is not kindness, it is martyrdom and it is not attractive.

I often say to my patients that if they can't look after themselves, they cannot possibly look after anyone else, because they simply will not be in a position to do so. They will be too tired and burnt out. Rather look after yourself well, and then you can look after others with vibrancy and love.

If your can't look after yourself, you cannot possibly look after anyone else

Kind Things

When I was very young, I decided that the world had too many nasty things in it for my liking, and these needed to be counterbalanced with "kind things" in order to make my life worth living. Kind things became a way of living which I still do with absolute relish. It involves anything which I consider to be deliciously self-indulgent and nourishing. This might be a beautiful bath oil, or planting a fragrant window box outside my bedroom window, or lying under a tree and looking at the sky through the filigree twigs, cuddling my dog, lying on my bed in the afternoon with a slice of cake, a pot of tea and a good book, cycling through the park at dusk listening to the deer bellowing in the autumn, going to bed at 6pm if I feel like it. Other people might like to go to the gym and then enjoy a hot steam.

It really doesn't matter, as long as your mind and body recognize that you are being kind to yourself. These little things in life matter. They do not involve great amounts of money but they bring great pleasure. The contentment that you get from "kind things" ripples from you like a wave of delight and you will find yourself encouraging others to find their own "kind things". Soon our lives focus on kindness, joy and contentment instead of stress and fatigue.

Redefine the way you see your illness

It may be that you have felt deeply exhausted for some time. Sad, frustrated and depressed. For hundreds of years spiritual teachers have referred to extended and particularly difficult times in our lives as The Dark Night of The Soul. These are not just little moments when you feel a bit sorry for yourself, but those few profound times in our lives when life rocks you to the core, and coming through it is fundamentally life-changing. It is as if you were a rat being shaken by the black dog of despair. The Dark Night of The Soul can rock you so deeply that even years afterwards, the memory can bring tears to one's eyes. It might sound incredibly crass to say that these can be very precious times, if only we can be guided into accepting these times as a temporary situation which has a very important purpose and will pass.

That is the trick to remember – it always passes, and it leaves you changed for the better. During these times, you might want to withdraw from people, and that is absolutely fine, because there is an instinctive urge to be alone and bury deep into yourself. This reconnection with yourself is the precious pearl. Sometimes in life it is necessary to allow yourself to sink right down to the bottom of the well, into the unknown depths, and there in amongst the mud and slime which is also a part of each of us, your hand groping in the mud, suddenly clasps the pearl which represents YOU, in all your natural iridescent beauty.

This is the real you, hidden away amongst the silt and mud, which represent the years of conditioning to which we have all been subjected. In that mud, our true talents and destinies are put aside, forgotten, and hidden from view. But if you can find within yourself the courage to drift down into the depths of yourself, and find the talent, the hobby, the vocation which makes you joyful, which fires your imagination and which makes your heart sing – then you have the opportunity to follow your own path towards a life where the real you shines so brightly again – just as you were born to do.

We were all born with something that made us shine. It is just that the vast majority of us got caught up in what we ought to do rather than what we want to do. This could be the time to be true to yourself and allow your soul to shine its own unique light on this Earth – so that you brighten it up a little for the rest of us.

I have often suggested to my patients that they consider their illness as a great gift. Of course, you can imagine that I do not always get a good response from this point of view, but I offer them the idea that they got to this place because of the way they lived their lives, or responded to life. This illness can be seen as a turning point, a time when you can reconsider the way you live your life, and a chance to re-imagine how you want to live.

Can you imagine this place you that have come to in your life as a gift and an opportunity to rediscover who you really are? Who is the real person under your skin, and what do you really want from life? Perhaps you could think of the illness as a rite of passage, an opportunity to take stock and reconsider your whole life ahead. In doing so, it can be seen as the chance to transform your relationship with life into one which is life sustaining and allows you to thrive with vigour and joy, not just survive.

Deep Peace

I have discussed balance many times through this book, and emphasized the balancing of the physical body, as well as your mental self. Many people find that profound illness caused by modern day stress acts as a catalyst for moving towards a more spiritual way of life. There are very many studies which show how the simple act of meditation or prayer realigns the mind to a much more peaceful state of being. Some people find that it is easier to connect with their spiritual self by slightly distracting their mental chatter with a gentle activity such as yoga, Tai Chi, or meditative walking in a forest. Others prefer to receive spiritual healing or Reiki, which helps to rebalance their energies and deepen their spiritual experience.

Many find that the moment the healer places his hands on their shoulders that they experience an intense release of emotion and the tears flow, releasing locked-in pain and allowing a deep sense of peacefulness to fill their being.

Your life maps

Sometimes it is difficult to see one's own life clearly, and to clearly acknowledge where we are spending too much energy or too little. Below is a simple map which can very quickly and clearly show you where you are spending too much energy and where you need to bring more focus into your life to achieve better balance.

- Do change the text in the bubbles to reflect your own experience of life.
- Imagine that you are grading yourself on a scale of 1 - 10, with 10 representing the most amount of time, and 0 representing no time.
- Imagine the scale running along each line running from the "Me" bubble to the activity bubble, with 0 starting at the edge of Me, ending at 10 on the edge of the outer bubble.
- Mark each line with a dot to represent how much time you think you spend with each scenario.
- Now join up the dots to create your own life pattern personal bubble.

See the example below.

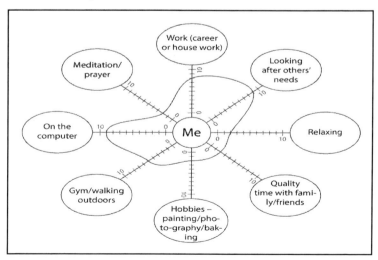

Having linked up the dots, you will notice that you do not have a perfect circle, but rather a wobbly circle, which will give you a very clear idea about the balance in the way you spend your time.

You can change the words to reflect your mental or emotional life, as the example below illustrates. As the whole point is to regain balance in your life, by highlighting the areas which are lacking, you can adjust your life accordingly so that when you do the map again, you find a more evenly balanced and fulfilled personal bubble.

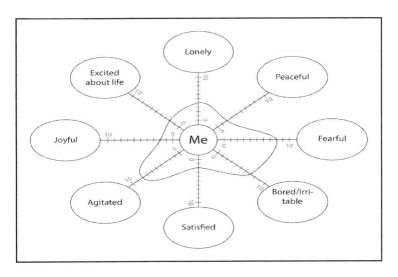

Chapter Seventeen

Living Well

We might ask ourselves how we as a society, or as a whole ever got into this mindset of working so hard, or living so stressfully that it actually makes us ill? We now are so embroiled in the culture of busyness that not only can we not see the wood for the trees – we don't even notice the beautiful trees! Stepping back a little to consider how we got here, we can gain a better perspective, and perhaps in doing so might choose another life-path, back towards a kinder, more humane way of living. Certainly, in choosing to live more gently, each one of us has the opportunity to demonstrate to younger people that it is possible to live well in a manner that is sustainable for our well-being, and that we don't have to live in a dog-eat-dog world in order to survive.

Living in a delusion

If you were to ask anyone, they would probably all agree that life seems so much faster paced and that people seem to be endlessly rushing about in these current times. In his book Finding Sanctuary [1], Abbot Christopher Jamison of Worth Abbey suggests that our predilection for busyness has come about as a result of Western governmental desire to grow the economy by maximising competition amongst businesses and people. Some writers even refer to the Western governmental neglect of care towards the genuine welfare of their citizens, as "farming the people" for financiers.

Nowadays, citizens are treated as consumers, and it is very difficult to escape this mind set because wherever we are, there are adverts brainwashing us into believing that we need to upgrade, replace and improve. The sometimes vicious competition at the school gate amongst the mums, and in the playground amongst the children is a very sad example. People can feel pressured into buying the latest "must have" thing, and we might ask – whatever happened to 'make do and mend'? The consumer is increasingly compelled to work longer and harder in order to acquire the money to fuel the consumeristic machine within which the modern mind is enslaved. Thus, we have become richer, busier, more stressed and sicker.

But why the stress? The fundamental drive of any living organism is self-preservation. As we are now, in general, so much wealthier than we have ever been in our entire human history, we should surely feel safer and more secure.

I propose that we are all so stressed because we have become almost entirely seduced by an illusion. The foundation upon which the illusion is built is a truth, and that is that one of the most basic human needs is to feel secure. To lose security or to worry about losing security is one of the greatest stresses we experience. But the illusion envelops us like a toxic fog, for we cannot see that we are seduced into the false belief that the more money we have – the more security we have.

This belief underpins our entire modern culture and is kept in securely place by powerful advertising and marketing strategies. We almost cannot help but believe that money will buy us the material goods and insurance policies which will keep us safe, protected from the storms of life, and satisfied. Thus, we race around, stressing out, burning up and ruining our health, trying to earn enough money to buy that security, all the time forgetting that without our health, we have nothing.

We spend most of our lives working very hard in the hope that one day we can retire with enough money to finally be able to do the things we want to do. Then we will be free. But in reality we are free already – except we have forgotten that. We are entangled within the chains of our cultural delusion, and that delusion keeps us on the hamster wheel, running round and round, exhausting ourselves.

You might be wondering what on Earth this has to do with burnout or fatigue. It has so much to do with these conditions, because most of the people I have treated with these illnesses have a history somewhere along the line of long term stress which burned them out. Living in a highly stressful world is not natural and is not the only way humans need to live, it is just the way which we, in the wealthy West, have come to believe is normal and acceptable. My argument is that in order to stay well, you might want to reconsider your life choices, so that they become more sustainable and self-nourishing.

Materialism in another time

A vivid account of the horrors of this blind belief in materialism is described in a letter to the King of Spain written in 1536 by Núñez Cabeza de Vaca, the Lord Treasurer of a Spanish expedition to America. The expedition was shipwrecked on the Florida coastline. Cabeza De Vaca and the three other survivors had absolutely no idea how to survive in this wild land. After some time they were taken in by the indigenous Americans, but when famine struck the Indians demanded that either they pay their way by healing the sick, or they would be pushed out of the community to fend for themselves. Not knowing anything about health plus with no medicines at their disposal, in desperation the Spanish men made the sign of the Cross over the sick, and prayed with all their hearts. Miraculously, the sick person recovered, and soon they were sent another, and then over time thousands of people were sent to these men to be blessed and healed.

The Indians rejoiced and with gratitude, fed and cared for the men, and passed them safely from tribe to tribe so that they made their way across the American continent towards Spanish-occupied America. The men were passed from tribe to tribes in peace where the tribes had once warred with each other, and so they left behind in their wake healing and peace. Eventually after eight years of living off the land with the tribes in a completely natural and sustainable manner, they reached Mexico. At this point, the Indians became exceedingly reticent about entering Spanish occupied territory. The Spanish, had of course, stolen their land for gold, and the Indians related how the Europeans had burned villages, destroyed the land and carried away half the men, and all the women and boys as slaves.

The four men finally joined their countrymen in Mexico, but found the experience shocking and revolting. Our narrator related in his letter to the king that *"The power of greed, the notions of conquest and slavery, and the desire for gold were tangible and repugnant to me. What kind of world will come from this I do not know, but this I can say: That greed and possession is not the way; that enslavement and destruction of the land will bring nothing but great sufferings; and that in creating a new world all things are possible but these things must be done from the spirit of the Christian heart."* [2]

The conquistadors were completely blinded by the materialistic delusion. They were mad for gold and would justify anything to get it. Cabeza de Vaca, the former Lord Treasurer, had been divorced long enough from that society for the scales to have fallen from his eyes and so that he could see the delusion clearly. Gold offers cold comfort.

Centuries of indoctrination have so blinded us in our faith that money buys security, that we feel sorry for and even guilty about the poor in Third World countries – but why? Because we judge them by our brainwashed point of view - money buys security, and that we are the lucky ones. Sick, exhausted and depressed, but lucky.

Thom Hartmann explains in his book The Last Hours of Ancient Sunlight [3], that the prime difference between "primitive" people and modern people is that the former generally have more leisure, virtually no crime, better psychological health, and a culture which holds as its primary values; cooperation and mutual respect as opposed to ours which holds competition and consumerism as indicators of wealth and therefore security.

Money poor - Heart rich

People in indigenous cultures are often money poor but heart rich. They share their food, the children have many mothers. Woe betide the man who attacks a woman, for all the women of the community go after him and beat him up. They make music together, dance together, grieve together, pray together, kill a goat and celebrate together. Nobody eats alone, and people are not usually lonely. They don't die alone. There is a system where when one has work, he shares his money with his community in the knowledge that if he loses his job, he in turn will be taken care of by the others. The elderly are venerable, and are respected as having wisdom and stories worth listening to. They do not have nor need a pension fund. Their grandchildren bounce on their old knees and in later years, these children take care of them. I know this because I come from Africa and I am describing a contemporary township life style. Let me be clear, I am not saying that life in the townships is ideal. Of course it is very far from that, but as a *community*, they do live more tribally and are often more supportive of each other than we are in our very independent lives. Alas, we have stolen from them their indigenous way of life and now of course, they have been rolled into our monied world, so there is crime and deprivation, but in general they are a happy bunch of people. In many respects, I envy them. Their people are tight around them. Is it not the ultimate security to know that your people will always be close to you, looking after you?

Perhaps in our contemporary independent lives, we have been

drawn away from the value of community. I suspect that most of us long to live within a nurturing group, and that we understand this is a warmer type of security.

Live naturally

What else is it that indigenous people do, and we don't do? They have a deep and nourishing relationship with nature and their land. All indigenous people have a rich connection with their land, and every creature or element which walks, crawls, swims and flies on it and above it. In their world view, every part of nature is vitalized and has a spirit or soul which the people honour and communicate with. This natural connection informs their lives, and fulfils them profoundly, in a way that unfortunately, we really cannot understand. Our modern society is suffering from a condition known as Nature Deficit Disorder and it is clear that our disconnection from the Earth is making humanity and our ecology seriously unhealthy. Our separation from nature has thrown our lives way out of balance and is utterly unsustainable, both on a human level and an environmental level. It hurts us in that our food and water is poisonous, our sources of fuel are running out, we cannot guarantee our grandchildren a healthy clean world, our air is filthy, we are not a vibrantly healthy population despite the abundance of food, and our souls are impoverished because our connection with nature is lost. Today Oxfam reported that one percent of the population holds half the world's wealth. We are so out of balance that our physical and soul health is suffering.

Have you ever noticed how energised you feel after a walk in the country? How satisfying it is to dig your gardening fingers into the soil, or the bracing feeling of standing on the beach with salty wind ripping through your hair? When we disconnect from the vital force of nature, we lose that revitalizing connection, and we suffer very badly. Nature literally re-vital-izes us – and without it, we become de-vitalized. So, what can we do to live more healthfully?

Be kind to yourself

Sometimes I suggest to a patient that she might think of herself as a small and confused child, somewhat battered by life and desperately tired. This little one needs love, care, nourishment, and nurturing back to the joy of life. How would you treat this child? Please, really do think about it. How would you treat her? Because this is how you need to be treated by yourself. Be kind to yourself. It really matters.

If we want to feel better, we need to live better

A young man once told a wise old man that he had fallen out of love with his wife and asked his advice. The sage told him *"Love her"*. Make an effort in the right direction and life will respond.

If we want to feel different in our lives, then we need to live differently. Kahil Gibran wrote in The Prophet *"Work is love made visible"*. Perhaps you could ask yourself: Do I look forward to going to work every day? Do I love how I spend my time? Do I love the company of my colleagues, clients, customers or friends? Or, do you just do what you do?

Can you envisage how different our society would be if we all earned our living by doing the work we love, rather than doing what we have to do to bring home the bacon? How joyous and more balanced our whole society could be. We would all be following our true paths, our hearts would sing. We would probably sing, and be more relaxed, happier and probably just as productive. There would probably be much more care towards all living beings, creativity and fun, music and beauty, laughter and co-operation.

Does this sound like a silly pipe dream? Why should it be? Many people live like this and yes, it is true that they often tend to earn less money, but overall they have enough for all the pleasures of life, and there is a great deal of satisfaction in their lives. So, it is happening already where the world consciousness is changing from the love of power towards the power of love. When we live with love, we live gently and kindly, and that nourishes life for all.

The balance of life

There are some communities around the world where you find people living full, healthy and active lives in their 80's, 90's and even 100's. These communities are not even all that remote – one such community lives in the pollution of Los Angeles and they are a religious community. What is it that these people are doing to maintain their apparent youthful vigour? Generally, it was found that these groups of people from different cultures around the world follow a similar lifestyle pattern:

- They move their bodies naturally – in other words, they walk and cycle, garden, sweep, dig. They are moving at a human pace, not speeding about at breakneck speed – achieving.
- They have a quiet time of the day where they meditate, pray, walk mindfully or spend time alone with themselves.
- They spend time in nature, and if possible in the sun collecting their vitamin D and all the cheerfulness that sunshine can bring.
- They have a purpose in their lives – something really matters to them, and it frequently involves a service to others. This gives their lives meaning.
- They spend time with their family, friends and loved ones. Family does not have to be blood relations. You can create a family through close bonds and regular contact with any other group of people. This creates a support network. Women tend to be better at this than men, but men's groups can offer a very supportive space where men can talk about things that they can't share with their wives. This is entirely natural in indigenous tribes – our group of hunters would be such an example. Modern soldiers in combat together also understand the value of a close group of men who they can rely on.

- They eat more vegetables, less meat, little refined carbohydrates, and cook from scratch.

What can we learn from these above points? Well, first of all, they are living naturally, as we were designed to live, like our tribesmen ancestors, or modern indigenous peoples. Importantly, they have balance in their lives. Some of us like to work for high velocity companies, whilst others prefer to work for ourselves. Either way it does not matter. What matters is balance. For instance, if you work very hard, take some time for yourself everyday. If your job is very mental, then do some physical exercise. If you are a carer, then join a group where you can talk about yourself. Take your holidays and have fun. Avoid those who draw too much energy from you without giving back. Make sure you eat a balanced diet, get enough rest, enough outdoor fun time, enough love. Really try to reconnect with nature – which is the greatest re-balancer of all.

Be kind to yourself
Be true to yourself
Reconnect with nature
Live with love

Chapter Eighteen

A last word

We have looked at the effect that stress has on our bodies, and how to repair that significant damage. I have also proposed how our cultural beliefs got us here in the first place, and offered suggestions as to how you might make another life choice, if you wish to. Finally, I would like to share my experience of what you can expect in the far future once you have recovered from adrenal exhaustion, M.E., CFS, burn-out or whatever category you may fall into.

During my years of helping people through this illness, I have found that people are never completely cured of illness caused by too much stress. Perhaps too much damage has been inflicted on the body, and there is always a weak point and vulnerability, or a cellular memory perhaps you could call it. This is why I emphasise the absolute importance of looking after yourself properly from this time forth, and forever more!

However, I can say clearly and emphatically that people do recover from this illness and live their lives fully without any symptoms of the illness. I am not God and cannot promise you a full recovery, much as I wish I could, but I can tell you that I have seen many many people recover very nicely from this illness.

I have a close friend who had ME and who took my herbal medicine until he recovered. Now, he lives a very full life, but when too much stress comes his way – he relapses. At first he used to panic and thought that he was stuck with M.E. again. I had to reassure him that he needs to rest and recover, take some herbs and eat properly, and that he will be fine again. This has happened several times, and now he understands the process and simply takes it really easy for a few weeks. Lo and behold, he recovers every time and then he is off again, roaring around happily on his Harley.

So you can live your life as if you are completely well, but you can never go back to the reckless wastage of energy which you might have done in the past. It is a bit like being more environmentally conscious – we are all thinking about sustainable energy these days. You will always need to hold an awareness of your limitations and always remember to be kind to yourself.

In a nutshell
If you have been ill from burn-out and are now on the road to recovery, please be aware that the recovery takes time. I find it takes from nine to twenty four months on average.

The recovery occurs in a step-wise manner, with two steps forward and one step back. Don't worry when you have a step backwards – that is completely natural, because the overall trend is upward. It is a bit like the housing market – there are blips, but over all, the house prices are going up.

If you do have a relapse, then have the good sense to take extra care of yourself until you recover – which you will.

You will find that the sooner you surrender into realising that you have to respect your body and your energy, the quicker you will recover. You absolutely cannot bust your way out of this illness. You will not get better this way, I cannot emphasise that enough.

In the early stages of the recovery program, my patients might have just one day when suddenly they feel well again. They might get really excited, but then very disappointed because the next day they feel unwell again. This is a wonderful moment, because I have consistently found that once people feel the sense of well-being even for just one day, they will after a while start to feel that healthy, most of the time.

I wish you the very best of health, a happy life, and kindness and joy every day.

References

Chapter Six
How stress makes us ill

1. Scotta L et al. Small adrenal glands in chronic fatigue syndrome: a preliminary computer tomography study. Psychoneuroendocrinology. 1999 Oct; 24(7):759-68
2. Tsigosa C, Chrousosb G, Hypothalamic-pituitary-adrenal axis, neuroendocrine factors and stress. J Psychosom Res. 2002 Oct;53(4):865-71
3. Patarcar R. Cytokines and Chronic Fatigue Syndrome. Ann N Y Acad Sci. 2001 Mar;933:185-200
4. Skowera, A et al. High levels of type 2 cytokine-producing cells in chronic fatigue syndrome. Clin Exp Immunol. 2004 Feb;135(2):294-302
5. Gur1 A et al. Hypothalamic-pituitary-gonadal axis and cortisol in young women with primary fibromyalgia: the potential roles of depression, fatigue, and sleep disturbance in the occurrence of hypocortisolism. Ann Rheum Dis. 2004;63:1504-1506
6. Parker J R et al. The neuroendocrinology of chronic fatigue syndrome and fibromyalgia. Psychological Medicine. 31, pp 1331-1345
7. Crofford L J et al. Basal circadian and pulsatile ACTH and cortisol secretion in patients with fibromyalgia and/or chronic fatigue syndrome. Brain, Behavior, and Immunity, Volume 18, Issue 4, July 2004, Pages 314-325
8. Wright R J. Stress and atopic disorders. Journal of Allergy and Clinical Immunology, Volume 116, Issue 6, December 2005, Pages 1301-1306

9. Elenkov I J, B, Chrousos G P, Stress Hormones, Th1/Th2 patterns, Pro/Anti-inflammatory Cytokines and Susceptibility to Disease. Trends in Endocrinology & Metabolism, Volume 10, Issue 9, 1 November 1999, Pages 359-368

10. Poanta L et al. Professional stress and inflammatory markers in physicians. Rom J Intern Med. 2010;48(1):57-63

11. Black P H, Glarbutt LD. Stress, inflammation and cardiovascular disease. Journal of Psychosomatic Research, Volume 52, Issue 1, January 2002, Pages 1-23

12. Abumadini S et al. Life events stress in ulcerative colitis: A case-control study. Saudi Journal of Gastroenterology, Vol 8, Issue 2, Pages 53-58

13. Davis M C et al. Chronic Stress and Regulation of Cellular Markers of Inflammation in Rheumatoid Arthritis: Implications for Fatigue. Brain Behav Immun. 2008 January; 22(1): 24-32

14. Cleare A J et al. Contrasting neuroendocrine responses in depression and chronic fatigue syndrome. Journal of Affective Disorders, Volume 34, Issue 4, 18 August 1995, Pages 283-289

15. Stokes P. The potential role of excessive cortisol induced by HPA hyperfunction in the pathogenesis of depression. European Neuropsychopharmacology, Volume 5, Supplement 1, 1995, Pages 77-82

16. Gustavo E et al. Enhancement of serotonin uptake by cortisol: A possible link between stress and depression. Cognitive, Affective, & Behavioral Neuroscience, Volume 1, Number 1, 96-104

17. Lupien S J et al. Cortisol levels during human ageing predict hippocampal atrophy and memory deficit. Nature Neuroscience 1, 69 - 73 (1998)

18. Prevelic G M et al. 24-hour serum Cortisol profiles in women with polycystic ovary syndrome. Gynecol Endocrinol. 1993 Sep;7(3):179-84

19. Tsilchorozidout et al. Altered Cortisol Metabolism in

Polycystic Ovary Syndrome: Insulin Enhances 50-Reduction But Not the Elevated Adrenal Steroid Production Rates. J Clin Endocrinol Metab. 2003 Dec;88(12):5907-13

20. Cahill C A. Differences in cortisol, a stress hormone, in women with turmoil-type premenstrual symptoms. Nurs Res. 1998 Sep-Oct;47(5):278-84

21. Nepomnaschy P A et al. Cortisol levels and very early pregnancy loss in humans. Proc Natl Acad Sci U S A. 2006 March 7; 103(10): 3938-3942

22. Negro-Vilar A, Stress and Other Environmental Factors Affecting Fertility in Men and Women. Environmental Health Perspectives Supplements 101 (Suppl. 2): 59-64 (1993)

Chapter Seven
No-Oh-Noo!

1. Pall, Martin L. Explaining "unexplained illnesses": disease paradigm for chronic fatigue syndrome, multiple chemical sensitivity, fibromyalgia, post-traumatic stress disorder, Gulf War syndrome, and others. Haworth Medical, 2007

2. http://www.thetenthparadigm.org/

3. Matsumoto K et al. Psychological stress-induced enhancement of brain lipid peroxidation via nitric oxide systems and its modulation by anxiolytic and anxiogenic drugs in mice. Brain Res. 1999 Aug 21;839(1):74-84

4. Vecchiet J et al. Relationship between musculoskeletal symptoms and blood markers of oxidative stress in patients with chronic fatigue syndrome. Neurosci Lett. 2003 Jan 2;335(3):151-4

Chapter Nine
Diet and blood sugar

1. Wilson, James L. Adrenal Fatigue: The 21st Century Stress Syndrome. Smart Publications, c2001
2. http://www.adrenalfatigue.org/

Chapter Eleven
Restoring the Adrenal Glands

1. Kroes BH et al. Inhibition of human complement by beta-glycyrrhetinic acid. Immunology. 1997 Jan;90(1):115-20
2. Fiore C et al. Antiviral effects of Glycyrrhiza species. Phytother Res. 2008 Feb;22(2):141-8
3. Wolkerstorfer A et al. Glycyrrhizin inhibits influenza A virus uptake into the cell. Antiviral Res. 2009 Aug;83(2):171-8
4. Lee B et al. Rehmannia glutinosa ameliorates scopolamine-induced learning and memory impairment in rats. J Microbiol Biotechnol. 2011 Aug;21(8):874-83
5. Kimura Y, Sumiyoshi M. Effects of various Eleuthrococcus senticosus cortex on swimming time, natural killer activity and corticosterone levels in forced swimming stressed mice. J Ethnopharmacol. 2004 Dec;95(2-3):447-53
6. Bohn B et al. Flow-cytometric studies with eleuthrococcus extract as an immunomodulatory agent. Arzneimittelforschung. 1987 Oct;37(10):1193-6
7. Bhattacharya S, Muruganandam A. Adaptogenic activity of Withania somnifera: an experimental study using a rat model of chronic stress. Pharmacol Biochem Behav. 2003 Jun;75(3):547-55
8. Mahdi A et al. Withania somnifera improves semen quanlity in stress related male fertility. Evid Based Complement Alternat Med. 2009 Sep 29
9. Khan S, et al. Molecular insight into the immune up-

regulatory properties of the leaf extract of Ashwagandha and identification of Th1 immunostimulatory chemical entity. Vaccine. 2009 Oct 9;27(43):6080-7

10. Malik F et al. Immune modulation and apoptosis induction: Two sides of antitumoural activity of a standardised herbal formulation of Withania somnifera. Eur J Cancer. 2009 May;45(8):1494-509

11. Panossian A et al. Rosenroot (Rhodiola rosea): traditional use, chemical composition, pharmacology and clinical efficacy. Phytomedicine 2010 Jun;17(7):481-93

12. van Diermen D et al. Monoamine oxidase inhibition by Rhodiola rosea L. roots. J Ethnopharmacol, 2009 Mar 18;122(2):397-401

13. Darbinyan V et al. Rhodiola rosea in stress induced fatigue--a double blind cross-over study of a standardized extract SHR-5 with a repeated low-dose regimen on the mental performance of healthy physicians during night duty. Phytomedicine, 2000 Oct;7(5):365-71

14. Lishmanov I et al. The cardioprotective and antiadrenergic activity of an extract of Rhodiola rosea in stress: Eksp Klin Farmakol 1994 Nov-Dec;57(6):61-3

15. The Herball; or Generall Historie of Plantes. Gathered by John Gerarde of London, Master in Chirugerie. Imprinted at London by John Norton, 1597. (Of Borage. Chap.269, pp 652-654)

Chapter Thirteen
Rebalance the immune system

1. Krawitz C et al. Inhibitory activity of a standardized elderberry liquid extract against clinically-relevant human respiratory bacterial pathogens and influenza A and B viruses. BMC Complement Altern Med. 2011 Feb 25;11:16

2. Meruelo D et al. Therapeutic agents with dramatic antiretroviral activity and little toxicity at effective doses:

aromatic polycyclic diones hypericin and pseudohypericin. Proc Natl Acad Sci U S A, 1988 Jul;85(14):5230-4

3. Pang L et al. In vitro anti-hepatitis B virus effect of Hypericum perforatum. J Huazhong Univ Sci Technolog Med Sci, 2010 Feb;30(1):98-102

4. Kubin A et al. Hypericin--the facts about a controversial agent. Curr Pharm Des 2005;11(2):233-53

5. Maury W et al. Identification of light-independent inhibition of human immunodeficiency virus-1 infection through bioguided fractionation of Hypericum perforatum. Virol J. 2009 Jul 13;6:101

6. Sun Y, Yang J. Experimental study of the effect of Astragalus membranaceus against herpes simplex virus type 1. Di Yi Jun Yi Da Xue Xue Bao, 2004 Jan;24(1):57-8

7. Kuo Y et al. Astragalus membranaceus flavonoids (AMF) ameliorate chronic fatigue syndrome induced by food intake restriction plus forced swimming. J Ethnopharmacol 2009 Feb 25;122(1):28-34

8. Cho W, Leung K. In vitro and in vivo immunomodulating and immunorestorative effects of Astragalus membranaceus. J Ethnopharmacol. 2007 Aug 15;113(1):132-41

9. Zhang Z et al. Effect of astragaloside on cardiomyocyte apoptosis in murine coxsackievirus B3 myocarditis. J Asian Nat Prod Res. 2007 Mar; 9(2):145-51

10. Micol V et al. The olive leaf extract exhibits antiviral activity against viral haemorrhagic septicaemia rhabdovirus (VHSV), Antiviral Research, Volume 66, Issues 2-3, June 2005, Pages 129-136

11. Pereira A et al. Phenolic Compounds and Antimicrobial Activity of Olive (Olea europaea L. Cv. Cobrançosa) Leaves. Molecules 2007, 12(5), 1153-1162.

12. Cannell J et al. Epidemiology and Infection, Epidemiology and Infection Cambridge University Press, (2006), 134: pp 1129-1140

13. Holick M, Chen T. Vitamin D deficiency: a worldwide

problem with health consequences, American Journal of Clinical Nutrition, Vol. 87, No. 4, 1080S-1086S, (April 2008)

14. Clara B et al. Differential effect of Coriolus versicolor (Yunzhi) extract on cytokine production by murine lymphocytes in vitro. International Immunopharmacology, Volume 4, Issue 12, Nov 2004, Pg 1549-1557

15. Borisov S. Cytokine Th1 to Th2 shift can be reversed by Coriolus versicolor supplementation. Prospective trial for HPV control by Coriolous versicolor. Clinical Journal of Mycology vol 1, 2012

16. Powell M, Medical Mushrooms A Clinical Guide, Mycology Press, 2010

Chapter Fourteen
Re-invogorating cellular energy

1. Tata, D and Yamamoto, B. Interactions between methamphetamine and environmental stress: role of oxidative stress, glutamate and mitochondrial dysfunction. Addiction, 102: 49-60

2. Seo J et al. Behavioral stress causes mitochondrial dysfunction via ABAD up-regulation and aggravates plaque pathology in the brain of a mouse model of Alzheimer disease. Free Radic Biol Med, 2011 Jun 1;50(11):1526-35

3. Fujita C et al. Direct effects of corticosterone on ATP production by mitochondria from immortalized hypothalamic GT1-7 neurons. J Steroid Biochem Mol Biol, 2009 Oct;117(1-3):50-5

4. Chen Y et al. Psychological stress alters ultrastructure and energy metabolism of masticatory muscle in rats. J Biomed Biotechnol. 2010

5. Lobanov S et al. Morphofunctional changes in mitochondria during stress. Bull Exp Biol Med 2007 Dec;144(6):849-52

6. Ramadan G et al. Anti-inflammatory and anti-oxidant properties of Curcuma longa (turmeric) versus Zingiber

officinale (ginger) rhizomes in rat adjuvant-induced arthritis. Inflammation, 2011 Aug;34(4):291-301

7. Rastogi M et al. Curcuminoids modulates oxidative damage and mitochondrial dysfunction in diabetic rat brain. Free Radic Res 2008 Nov;42(11-12):999-1005

8. Sarvalkar P et al. Antioxidative effect of curcumin (Curcuma longa) on lipid peroxidation and lipofuscinogenesis in submandibular gland of D-galactose- induced aging male mice. Journal of Medicinal Plants Research Vol. 5(20), pp. 5191-5193, 30 September, 2011

9. Panossian A et al. The Adaptogens Rhodiola and Schizandra Modify the Response to Immobilization Stress in Rabbits by Suppressing the Increase of Phosphorylated Stress-activated Protein Kinase, Nitric Oxide and Cortisol. Wikman, Drug Target Insights. 2007; 2: 39-54

10. Chen N et al. Schisandrin B enhances cerebral mitochondrial antioxidant status and structural integrity, and protects against cerebral ischemia/reperfusion injury in rats. Biol Pharm Bull, 2008 Jul;31(7):1387-91

11. Sin P et al. Effect of a Lignan-Enriched Extract of Schisandra Chinensis on Aflatoxin B1 and Cadmium Chloride-Induced Hepatotoxicity in Rats. Pharmacology & Toxicology vol 78, Issue 6, pg 413-416, June1996

12. Haraguchi H et al. Inhibition of lipid peroxidation and superoxide generation by diterpenoids from Rosmarinus officinalis. Planta Med. 1995 Aug;61(4):333-6

13. Soria Freozo C et al. Expression of NMDA receptor subunits in rat prefrontal cortex with CCL4-induced hepatic damage after a treatment with Rosmarinus officinalis L. Neurologia 2012 Jan 2

14. Sagorchev P et al. Investigations into the specific effects of rosemary oil at the receptor level. Phytomedicine 2010 Jul;17(8-9):693-7

15. Yamamoto J et al. Testing various herbs for antithrombotic effect. Nutrition, 2005 May;21(5):580-7

16. Ventura-Martinez R et al. Spasmolytic activity of Rosmarinus officinalis L. involves calcium channels in the guinea pig ileum. J Ethnopharmacol, 2011 Oct 11;137(3):1528-32

17. Black C et al. Ginger (Zingiber officinale) reduces muscle pain caused by eccentric exercise. J Pain, 2010 Sep;11(9):894-903

18. Iranloye B et al. Anti-diabetic and anti-oxidant effects of Zingiber Officinale on alloxan-induced and insulin-resistant diabetic male rats. Niger J Physiol Sci, 2011 Nov 23;26(1):89-96

19. Heeba G, Abd-Elghany M. Effect of combined administration of ginger (Zingiber officinale Roscoe) and atorvastatin on the liver of rats. Phytomedicine, 2010 Dec 1;17(14):1076-81

20. Prevoo D et al. The Effect of Sutherlandia frutescens on Steroidogenesis: Confirming Indigenous Wisdom. Endocrine Research, 2004, Vol. 30, No. 4, Pages 745-751.

21. Prevoo D et al. The influence of Sutherlandia frutescens on adrenal steroidogenic cytochrome P450 enzymes, Journal of Ethnopharmacology, Volume 118, Issue 1, 19 June 2008, Pages 118-126.

22. Fernandes A et al. The antioxidant potential of Sutherlandia frutescens, Journal of Ethnopharmacology, Volume 95, Issue 1, November 2004, Pages 1-5.

23. van Wyke B, Gerike N. People's Plants. Briza Publications, 2000.

24. Wattanathorn J et al. Positive modulation of cognition and mood in the healthy elderly volunteer following the administration of Centella asiatica. J Ethnopharmacol, 2008 Mar 5;116(2):325-32.

25. Kumar A et al. Neuroprotective Effects of Centella asiatica against Intracerebroventricular Colchicine-Induced Cognitive Impairment and Oxidative Stress. Int J Alzheimers Dis, 2009 Sep 13;2009. pii: 972178.

26. Powell M, Medical Mushrooms A Clinical Guide, Mycology Press, 2010

27. Kumar R et al. Cordyceps sinensis promotes exercise endurance capacity of rats by activating skeletal muscle metabolic regulators. J Ethnopharmacol, 2011 Jun 14;136(1):260-6.
28. Ko K and Leung H. Enhancement of ATP generation capacity, antioxidant activity and immunomodulatory activities by Chinese Yang and Yin tonifying herbs. Chinese Medicine, vol 2.

Chapter Sixteen
Staying Well

1. Lipton, Bruce H. The biology of belief: unleashing the power of consciousness, matter & miracles. Hay House, 2008

Chapter Seventeen
Living Well

1. Jamison, Christopher. Finding sanctuary: monastic steps for everyday life. Weidenfeld & Nicolson, 2006
2. Feldman, Christina and Kornfield, Jack. Stories of the spirit, stories of the heart: parables of the spiritual path from around the world. Harper, 1991
3. Hartmann, Thom. The last hours of ancient sunlight: waking up to personal and global transformation. Harmony Books, 2001

Manufactured by Amazon.ca
Bolton, ON